SetFree

"He lifted me out of the slimy pit,
out of the mud and mire;
he set my feet on a rock
and gave me a firm place to stand.

"He put a new song in my mouth,
a hymn of praise to our God.
Many will see and fear
and put their trust in the LORD."

—Psalm 40:2, 3, NIV

Set Free

Michael and Amber

Harris's story of

miraculous recovery

and forgiveness

MICHAEL and AMBER HARRIS
with James Ponder

Pacific Press® Publishing Association
Nampa, Idaho
Oshawa, Ontario, Canada
www.pacificpress.com

Designed by Linda Griffith
Cover photo composite by Amber Harris and Linda Griffith
Photography by Jim Paliungas

Additional copies of this book are available by
calling toll free 1-800-765-6955 or visiting
http://www.adventistbookcenter.com.

ISBN:0-8163-2039-X

04 05 06 07 08 • 5 4 3 2 1

Dedication

To the Son of Man,

who was bruised, crushed, forsaken, and destroyed

to bring us to the heart of the Father,

whose arms are open wide to all,

whatever their sorrows, addictions, disabilities, or despair . . .

and to everyone

who struggles to know the truth and to be set free.

Acknowledgments

We wish to thank Marsha and Rick Claus for encouraging us to write the story when we had just about given up. Thank you also to Anna Withers and her prayer warriors for supporting our ministry and for all their prayers for the book. Their prayers were answered.

—Michael and Amber Harris

My deepest appreciation to Michael and Amber Harris for openly sharing their painful journey from despair to freedom so others can go free. I couldn't have written this book without the prayers, love, and support of my beautiful wife, Lupe, or the wisdom, tough love, and tenacity of my mentor and dear friend Euel Atchley, who led me to Christ twenty-seven years ago. And love and blessings to all the members of my family in the United States and Peru and of God's family in heaven and on earth.

—James Ponder

Table of Contents

Foreword

One of the strangest events in the history of alternative medicine took place when a man who could neither hear nor speak was presented to a colorful folk healer with a controversial reputation for evaluation and treatment. Seeking help outside the ranks of the medical establishment isn't always advisable. Many alternative health practitioners are ethical and conscientious. However, as Alan Alda reported on an episode of the *Scientific American* television broadcast, a high percentage are opportunistic charlatans who capitalize on the sufferings of others.

The healer in question was already under investigation by the authorities at the time this incident took place. Despite the suspicions of the investigators, he was widely acclaimed not only for getting results but also for his unconventional methods. In this case the healer stuck his finger in the patient's ear and touched the man's tongue with his own saliva. Then the healer spoke the same strange word he would later say to my friend Michael Harris. He said, *"Ephphatha,"* which can be translated either "Open up" or "Be opened." According to eyewitness testimony, the speech-and-hearing-impaired man suddenly began talking and hearing for the first time in his life. People who knew him were amazed by the cure.

I felt a similar excitement the first time I heard Michael Harris sing. As I listened to the way he turned ordinary songs into deepwater expressions of the human soul, I was fairly certain he'd been taking professional voice training for decades. Imagine my surprise, then, when Michael insisted he'd only been singing for a few months and never had a voice lesson in his life.

That was in the early 1990s. Back then, neither he nor I could have possibly known that he would go on to become an internationally recognized recording artist with more than a dozen CDs to his credit or that he would one day hold standing-room-only concerts around the world.

The funny thing is that despite his fabulous voice, Michael never thought about devoting his life to making music until the Healer started dropping subtle little hints—as he did the day he told Michael to sing in a crowded outdoor marketplace. When Michael complied, traffic came to a sudden halt as folks of all ages gathered around to listen.

But that isn't the *really* big news of what the Healer did for Michael and Amber. When I heard the full story, I could hardly believe it myself. For starters, He saved them from a horrifying death in a bone-crushing, single-car accident on Interstate 15 en route to Las Vegas. Then, in one amazing step, He liberated Michael from helpless addiction to cocaine, marijuana, speed, and alcohol. After that, against seemingly insurmountable odds, He rebuilt Michael and Amber's fractured marriage. Compared with all that, the task of turning an underprivileged kid from the South Side of Chicago into a popular and respected Christian musician seems like nothing at all.

Before you proceed to the amazing story of how Michael almost killed Amber, his wife, and how the Healer salvaged their lives and gave them a brand-new reason for living, let me digress long enough to say that when Michael called to ask if I would help him write this book, I knew

I couldn't spare the time. Not only do I have a very demanding career, but my free time was occupied with the challenge of condensing my first novel from a seven-hundred-page monstrosity to a readable tome half that size. But the more I thought about it, the more I realized Michael and Amber's story had to be told. So I put *River Over the World* on hold until we could get this book off to Pacific Press®. "I should be able to knock it out in three or four months," I thought. Two years later, *River* still sits on my shelf. Nevertheless, I'm extremely glad I finally did agree to take this project on. I'm more convinced than ever that this story needs to be shouted from the mountain tops.

Michael and Amber's epic adventure reminds me of something the townspeople were asking about the Healer. "Who is this guy?" they want to know. "He does everything so well!"

I couldn't agree more!

James Lewis Ponder
Ventura, California
January 2004

Chapter One

Destined to Die

I was standing in a schoolyard on Chicago's famous South Side the day I was sentenced to die.

I was twelve years old, but in my heart, I felt cool and sophisticated beyond words. With my girlfriend by my side and a cigarette dangling casually from my lips, I convinced myself I was already a man. Tough, cynical, and confident, I knew I could hang with the best.

From out of nowhere, a guy I didn't like walked up and asked me for a cigarette. "I don't smoke," I said.

He snatched the cigarette from my mouth, and immediately, I punched him hard in his. I wasn't about to take such a calloused affront to my dignity without a serious fight—especially not in front of my girl.

As he slunk away, rubbing his jaw in defeat, I laughed out loud. "I won!" I gloated. Needless to say, my lady was impressed.

I forgot about the fight until later that evening, when I went out to help one of my pals move into a new place. Most of the streetlights were out in our part of the city, but after a moment or two, my eyes adjusted to the light. As I walked down the street, I noticed a couple of guys heading my way in the darkness. Only when they got up close could I see that they were grinning from ear to ear.

Then I saw that one of them was the kid from the skirmish in the playground that afternoon. Why was he smiling like that? His buddy, a large man at least twice my age, affected an idiotic grin as he lunged and grabbed me by the throat. Before I knew what was happening, he was slapping me around, and I was trying hard to figure out what I could possibly do to escape serious injury.

I knew I was in trouble when the big guy shoved me between two parked cars and threw me into oncoming traffic. I jumped back just in time to avoid certain death. But they kept at it. Every time I struggled out of the street, cruel fists knocked me backward into the flow of traffic.

I have no idea how long the fist-ducking and car-dodging actually went on; it seemed like an eternity to me. I thought my heart would burst if a car didn't squash me first. Was I destined to die on the street in front of my friend's house? I hoped not! I knew I couldn't hold out much longer, but nobody was coming to my rescue, and I wasn't about to go down easy!

All of a sudden I realized the fighting had stopped. Were they as worn out as I was? Had they grown tired of the struggle and decided it wasn't fun anymore? Had they underestimated the strength of my will to survive?

As it turned out, they were merely getting ready for round two. It began when they hauled me into a dark alley beside the house.

This is the moment of truth! I thought to myself. *They're gonna kill me out here in the alley, and nobody will find me until morning. I'm a goner!*

Murder isn't rare on the South Side of Chicago. It happens every day of the year. Sometimes it's a drug deal gone bad; sometimes a guy catches his wife with another man. More often than not, however, it's just a gang romp turned deadly. When you read about it in the paper or see it on TV, it's easy to shake your head and say, "What a shame!" But when you're the one about to get carved up or shot in the head, it's an entirely different experience altogether! *Run for it, Michael!* I thought to myself. *Run, man, run!*

But the moment I mustered the strength to escape, the big guy slammed me up against the wall and reached inside his coat for a gun. As he raised the gun to my head, I opened my mouth to scream bloody murder, but I couldn't make a sound.

"This is it, Michael!" said a loud voice inside. *"This is the end of your life!"*

The sound of the safety lock clicking into the off position on a pistol takes on a terrifying aspect when someone is ramming the barrel of the gun very hard into your temple. I clenched both fists with all my might, gritted my teeth, and prepared to die.

This can't be happening! I thought to myself. *I'm nowhere near prepared to die! Somebody help me!*

As the history of my life raced in an adrenalized, dervishlike fury before my eyes, I caught sight of a third figure lunging down the alley towards me. Excitement shot through my veins as the pump in my chest accelerated to several hundred beats a minute. Was this new guy coming to join in the kill? Did he have a knife? Was I going to be cut to ribbons and stabbed through the heart before they finally pulled the trigger and finished me off?

"Mike, is that you?" I heard a familiar voice shouting from the street entrance to the alley. "Hey!" the guy yelled in booming, authoritative tones. "Leave my friend alone!"

In the fastest maneuver of my entire life, I wrenched myself free from my intended assassins and ran out of there with every ounce of energy that remained in my body. God had just saved my life, and I wasn't about to stick around and discuss the formalities or talk about the weather.

I flew down the block like a lightning bolt, dodging cars and pedestrians until I leaped across the driveway to my own front lawn and shot up the stairs. In one frantic motion, I jerked the door open, flung myself inside, slammed it shut without even turning around, and raced upstairs to my room. Once there, I doubled over at the waist and gasped for air. My head was pounding, my sides were splitting with pain, blasts of adrenalin were surging through my veins, and every heaving breath was a desperate gulp for survival.

People who survive close encounters with their own mortality often testify that their lives are never the same after the incident. They say everyday events take on new significance; that the simple act of drawing a breath becomes a sacrament of unexpected meaning. That's precisely *not* how it was for me. My first thought was, *What on earth am I gonna tell my mom?*

I could think of several good reasons for not telling her the truth. A few months earlier, I had personally witnessed a nasty incident in which a brave young mother was nearly killed by gang members simply because she stepped in to defend her kid from their cowardly assault. I wouldn't expose my mom to that kind of danger for anything.

The atmosphere in gang-infested neighborhoods is always tense and dangerous. Even though I had wanted to come to that poor woman's aid, I knew it could cost me my life, so I pretended not to see a thing.

Fortunately for her, the psychopathic bullies inexplicably backed down and walked away.

Now that I had been the subject of a brutal assault, I wasn't about to tell my mother what had happened and place her in jeopardy. I knew exactly what she would do if she found out: She'd march right out there in the middle of the night and confront my assailants without batting an eye. If they didn't shoot her outright, they would certainly mark our family for cruel retaliation and revenge. Gangsters can be sadistic beyond reason. They might rape my sisters or toss a Molotov cocktail into our living room just for fun.

What could I tell Mama? She would see the blood running down my face, and there was no way to hide the swelling and the bruises, so I had to come up with a story and fast!

By the time I heard her footsteps coming up the stairs, my alibi was all fleshed out and ready to go. Muhammad Ali was the hero of all the kids in the neighborhood. So we used to take turns pummeling the starch out of each other in a boxing ring we had set up in a vacant lot, and it wasn't particularly uncommon for kids to stagger home from the ring in pretty bad shape after a few rounds of sparring; I just hoped Mother wouldn't notice how far my condition exceeded the usual quota of bumps and bruises.

"They really got the best of me tonight," I said, hoping she'd take the bait. I hated lying to my mother, but I hated the thought of watching her die a whole lot more.

"Did they ever!" she exclaimed, giving my wounds a thorough going over with her eyes. "Come on, Michael. Let's get you cleaned up."

That night I lay on my bed rehearsing everything in my mind. Long after the lights went out and everybody else was fast asleep, my heart was still pounding and I felt like I was flying. Against great odds, I was still alive. And to my amazement, my mom had bought the explanation without pressing me for details.

I'll never forget the desperate terror I experienced that night. It was the first time I survived a close brush with death. It wouldn't be the last, though. The next encounter would take place halfway between Barstow, California, and Las Vegas, Nevada, in the middle of the worst night of my life. I would be driving on the other side of ninety miles an hour, soaring high on cocaine and speed, and literally crashing and burning on the edge of oblivion.

Once again, I would be hurtling over the brink—racing toward the big lights out.

Chapter Two

The Two Strongest Women in the World

Working in a bar on the South Side of Chicago is hardly the sort of career an intelligent young woman dreams of attaining, yet that was the employment opportunity Pearly Mae Harris accepted for herself when I was eight.

Did my mother have a choice? Sometimes I wonder. I'm sure she had bigger goals and dreams than serving alcoholic beverages in a run-down tavern, but even though her work was often depressing and demeaning— not to mention dangerous as she broke up fights and soothed wounded egos—I never heard her complain. Not even once.

Mother and I always shared a special bond. I was born in Indianapolis, Indiana, on August 20, a day that just happened to be her birthday as well. She always said I was her birthday gift. I always felt loved and affirmed whenever she said that.

I was the third of Mother's seven children. My two older sisters, Gloria Stean and Virginia Ann, used to taunt me with a little ditty they made up: "First there was Stean, then there was Ann, then there was Michael in a garbage can!"

I never particularly liked that line about my place of origin, but I still enjoyed the attention. Stean, as we called Gloria, and Ann looked enough alike to be sisters, but I didn't look like either of them. I used to wonder why. A bit later on, we were joined by another sister, Sonja, and our brother,

Robert. Baby Levette didn't arrive on the scene for several more years. Altogether, there were four different fathers in our family, although in reality, our mother filled the roles of both father and mother for all of us.

Mother was our only means of survival. She worked her fingers to the bone, as the saying goes, to make sure we had everything we needed. And although we lived in one of the poorest parts of town, we never lacked food, shelter, or nice clothes to wear. Mother gets an A+ for the way she raised us.

Her sister was also a jewel. Known to us kids as Aunt Ree, Mother's sister, Margaret, lived in Chicago. She was a real blessing to our family and came to visit us as often as she could. And every time she came, she brought gifts for each of us. In a very real sense, Aunt Ree was the spiritual backbone of our large, extended family. Her personality was beautiful and expansive; I couldn't help liking her. She radiated such kindness that everyone could plainly see she loved Jesus with all her heart and soul.

As with Mama, I enjoyed a special connection to Aunt Ree. She was always careful to shower love and affection on all us kids, but I knew she took a particular liking to me. I was very excited when, at the end of one of Aunt Ree's visits to our home, she told Mother she couldn't bear the thought of leaving me. "Could Michael please go with me to Chicago?" she pleaded. I was overjoyed when Mother said Yes. Even though I was only five, I threw myself into the task of packing my bags. I could hardly wait to go!

When we finally arrived in Chicago, I became aware of a dark cloud that hung over my aunt and uncle. Their seventeen-year-old son, Joseph, had died a few months before I came to stay with them. After suffering massive injuries when he fell off the back of a truck, Joseph developed cancer and never recovered. Aunt Ree and Uncle were heartbroken. Although I knew I could never replace their own child, I believe my coming to live with them offered some comfort and distraction from their deep pain at the loss of their son.

Aunt Ree was a homemaker in the best sense of the word. Since she didn't have to work, she stayed home and kept the place like a castle. And could she cook! I'll never forget her mouth-watering fried chicken served with mashed potatoes, collard greens, and sweet potato pie. I better change the subject before I get too hungry to finish telling my story!

We called my uncle by his initials, A.C. He worked hard in the steel mill to provide a good home for his family and give Auntie just about everything she wanted. Growing up within the circle of their love, I never imagined how enormously positive an influence Auntie and Uncle would exert on my life later on.

Aunt Ree took us to church almost every day of the week for classes and services. Good thing, too! I knew almost nothing about spiritual values, but I learned a lot from the sermons and hymns in church.

I also learned something about discipline! One day, as I was sitting in the back row with the other kids, Aunt Ree suddenly noticed that I was getting a bit too noisy. She took me to the back room and tanned my hide. Dr. Spock might argue that she deprived me of self-expression, but I believe she taught me to respect authority, especially in God's house. After that, I was the quietest kid in church.

I was attending an elementary school on the south side of town. My peers enjoyed my mischievous antics, and spurred on by their encouragement, I became increasingly disrespectful of my teacher. One day I decided to put on a rodeo in the classroom for the benefit of the other kids. They readily joined in, and before long, the whole place erupted into a ruckus of major proportions. We were riding each others' backs and whooping it up!

However, A.C. didn't seem particularly impressed with my antic creativity when he picked me up from the principal's office that afternoon. In fact, he didn't say a word all the way home. Once we got there, he let his fingers do the talking, and I got one of the strongest hidings of my entire career. The lesson stuck with me all my life. Ever afterward, I became considerably more obedient and respectful of authority.

Aunt Ree had an incredible singing voice. As she sang praises to God, accompanying herself on the tambourine, I used to imagine that I could see the notes flowing from the tips of her toes all the way up and out through her mouth. Even when I was a five-year-old, her music blessed my heart and soul. I can only imagine what her gift must have meant to others. And she was a powerful singer! In my professional opinion, she was every bit the equal of Mahalia Jackson. If you've ever heard that gospel singer, you have a pretty clear idea of just how good my auntie sounded.

I'll never forget my first Christmas with Aunt Ree and Uncle. My eyes were wide with anticipation as we went from store to store, picking out toys and goodies for all the kids. They brought a family friend along to distract me when they shopped for my presents. I was so busy absorbing all the joys and wonders of the Christmas season that I didn't have a clue what was happening on my behalf.

At precisely 1 A.M. on December 25, Aunt Ree and A.C. woke me from sleep. I needed no second invitation! I bounced out of bed eager to open my presents. I was full of questions: What had they gotten me? Was it OK to rip the packages open, or did I have to be tidy about it? Could I play with my toys right then?

Another big part of the enjoyment was the appetizing aroma of oranges and apples that filled the room. There were walnuts and pecans, colorful wrapping paper, and angelic expressions on Auntie and Uncle's faces. It all added up to one of the most beautiful memories of my childhood. I still remember it plainly, right down to the scent of fresh snow wafting in through the window.

After three years, Mother couldn't bear the thought of living without me and my two older sisters, who had also come to live with Aunt Ree and Uncle. So when I was eight, she joined us in Chicago. When she arrived, Mama introduced us to Sonja and Robert. We were delighted to be one great big happy family!

The only work Mother could find was the barmaid job at the tavern. The hours were horrible and the environment anything but inspiring, but Mother had five hungry children at home, and she threw herself into the job with all diligence and responsibility.

She rented an apartment directly over the bar. Living there was an education in itself! Day and night we could hear the bump and thump of the jukebox as well as the shouting and breaking of glass that marked the frequent fights.

Mother worked the midnight shift four times a week. It was hard work, and far beneath her dignity. She waited on lecherous, drunken customers, yet still managed to keep the peace and close the place down promptly at two in the morning.

Even so, she got little respect from her boss. He took advantage of her determination to work hard and do a good job by treating her with gross disrespect and dishonesty. He underpaid her at every opportunity.

Since Mother worked such long hours, she didn't have a lot of energy for meal planning and cooking. My sister Stean did her best, but after eating Aunt Ree's food, I was a difficult customer to please. Her heart was in the right place, however, and even though the food wasn't what I was used to, I knew she was doing her best. Nevertheless, we looked forward to the times when Mother brought hamburgers and barbecued ribs home from the tavern.

When Levette was born two years later, Mama decided it was time to move to a better place. Our new neighborhood near 75th and Union was every bit as gang infested as the area around the tavern, but at least we weren't living one floor up from a bar. The relative peace and quiet of our new surroundings was delicious.

By the time we moved into our new place, I was ten years old and ready to take on the world. I had no idea of the challenges I would face in learning to cope with the gangs.

Chapter Three

Living in a Horror Movie

At first, the Chicago street gangs left me alone. I knew they existed, heard about the horrible things they did, and understood that they were very dangerous, but for the most part, they left me alone.

That all changed in my tenth year of life. Suddenly I shot up to six feet tall and towered over my peers. Wherever I went, I stuck out like the gangly upstart I was, and gang members took my newfound height as license to confront me.

I quickly became adept at recognizing gang members by the way they dressed. The colors of their headbands differentiated between the neighborhood gangs in the same way that team colors separate Broncos fans from Raiders fans. Anytime I saw several members of the same gang assembling on a corner or in a back alley, I knew something was going down. I also knew it was time to get outta there fast!

By the time I turned twelve, I was in constant danger. I could hardly walk across the street without being accosted by the South Side gangs. I desperately tried to avoid them as I went to and from school each day but found it increasingly impossible to escape their harassment. I would be less than honest if I didn't confess that I was terribly afraid.

Unless you have been the subject of ongoing physical and verbal harassment, you have no idea how difficult it can be to maintain your composure. Imagine yourself as a twelve-year-old just trying to mind your own business. Maybe you're watching TV or doing your homework in the privacy of your own home when a gun blast shatters the atmosphere. You dive for cover under the bed or leap into a closet, hoping they aren't coming after you. And regardless of how hard you try to reassure yourself that it doesn't affect you, the presence of violence at every turn is unnerving and intimidating. From my bedroom window, I regularly saw guys getting beaten within an inch of their lives. I witnessed stabbings and shootings. I often saw people duck behind buildings to avoid capture and torture. More times than I care to recall, I saw people flung off tall buildings. I was terrified all the time; I felt like I was living in a horror movie.

Walking to school was a dangerous trek through a combat zone. I scrutinized every car that passed on the street to avoid being the target of a drive-by shooting. I kept an eye on what was happening two and three blocks ahead to make sure I wasn't walking into an ambush. Whenever I saw several guys walking down my side of the street, I whistled nonchalantly and crossed to the other side. If they followed, I had to make up my mind in the skip of a heartbeat: Should I stand and fight or run like the wind? More times than I care to remember, I got the daylights beaten out of me for making the wrong decision or for innocently strolling into the wrong place at the wrong time.

Police officers and politicians struggled to conquer the gangs, but the gangs, not the authorities, ruled the street. In fact, the Blackstone Rangers, the Vice Lords, and a huge gang called, ironically enough, the Disciples were the real movers and shakers of Chicago in the 1960s. By trafficking in narcotics, gambling, prostitution, extortion, and murder for hire, they controlled an enormous underground economy worth millions of dollars.

As a kid, I tried to resist the gangs, to "just say No" and make it stick. But when six or seven big guys step up and announce that you've just been drafted to help them rob a liquor store, there isn't a lot you can do but comply—not if you value your life!

When that happened to me, I would pretend to go along with the plan, but as soon as they entered the store, I would run away as fast as I could. I knew God didn't want me participating in such activities. Looking back, I can see that He was looking out for me all those years or I wouldn't be alive to tell the story today. But right then, in the life-and-death intensity of it all, it was hard to have a lot of faith. I calculated everything I did, every move I made, to ensure my survival.

Once you get drafted into a gang, it's almost impossible to get out with your life. You either remain loyal to the gang or face the severest consequences. One day a group of gangsters walked right into the classroom I was attending and said they'd come to see a gang member who just happened to be sitting right next to me. The teacher respectfully asked the gangsters to leave, but they slapped her around, then walked over to the kid they were looking for and beat him senseless. Then they threw him out the window and walked away. It made an enormous impression on everyone in the room!

Another terrifying incident took place at a birthday party for my cousins and me. We were inside the house enjoying the party when, for some reason or other, I decided to step outside. When I did, I found a bunch of older guys sitting on our front porch. That was fine. We knew them; they were guys from our neighborhood. But as I looked up the street, I saw a gang I didn't know approaching at a deliberate pace. They strolled up our sidewalk and asked the guys on the porch if they could come inside and join the party. Since their intentions were unknown, the request was denied.

The next thing I knew, one of the newcomers ran up onto the porch and pulled one of our neighborhood guys onto the lawn. As if on cue, the rest of the outsiders pounded the man with a baseball bat until he lay bloody and lifeless on the front lawn.

We all raced inside, hoping to shut the danger out. But no sooner had we slammed the door than bricks came smashing through the windows like bombs. It seemed like every window in the house shattered simultaneously. We were rolling all over the floor and ducking behind doors trying to escape the danger. To this day, I can still vividly feel the horrifying terror that shot through my heart. Things didn't quiet down until the police arrived several minutes later.

Of course, being selected for membership in a gang didn't mean you were out of harm's way. The gang leaders were always posing some kind of trial or initiation to make sure you were worthy of belonging. I'll never forget the first time I was coerced, completely against my will, to attend a meeting of the gang. I was taken to an abandoned building in a particularly dangerous part of town far away from the watchful eyes of the police. Once inside, I was escorted downstairs to a dingy basement, where the gang meeting was already in session.

Two lines of thirty to forty guys stood parallel to each other. The poor guy in the center was forced to walk up and down between them as they subjected him to every imaginable form of torture. Apparently he had done something to dishonor the organization; perhaps he had failed to carry out some appointed task or had been accused of betraying another member of the gang. Whatever the poor guy's mistake, he was viciously smashed and beaten from all sides. When he fell to the ground, every member of the gang jumped on him and pounded him to a pulp. By the time they finished, he was completely unconscious. I have no reason to believe he survived.

I've wracked my brain trying to figure out why ordinary men and boys can become so extraordinarily cruel and heartless; to understand why they feel it necessary to inflict such horrible suffering on their peers. The only "reasons" I can find are fear and hopelessness. The people I knew who were attracted to gang membership were psychological and emotional disasters long before they joined. Many of them showed symptoms of sadistic, psychopathic personalities. They were usually from broken homes, had known little if any love, and had received almost no moral guidance or constructive discipline from the adults in their lives. Some of them were born addicted to drugs or alcohol; others had been abandoned or physically and sexually abused from early childhood. The deck was stacked against them right from the start.

Regardless of how cruel and irrational the gangs can be, they provide several elements missing from the lives of misguided young men and women. That's how they fill their ranks. For kids from slummy apartments owned by corrupt landlords and filled with every form of vice and humiliation known to humanity, the promise of protection, recognition, and discipline seems too good to resist. For children accustomed to nothing but divorce, violence, and deterioration in every sphere of life, joining an organization that is a surrogate family, financial provider, and personal protector often seems like the only way to survive.

I believe that many young people who are marginalized and rejected by society are almost destined to become gangsters. The problem starts in the home environment. Like mine, their fathers are nowhere in sight. Their mothers often have to work two, three, and even more jobs just to survive and put food on the table. The combination of the parents' long hours away from their kids coupled with the fact that the kids are almost constantly exposed to a variety of enticing temptations comprises an almost foolproof formula for juvenile delinquency.

Another factor contributing to the moral decay in the lives of many young people from the streets is that very often, the most lucrative employment opportunities for women are in the fields of stripping, prostitution, and other X-rated forms of vice. It's nearly impossible to imagine the demoralizing influence their mother's employment identity has on the children of these women unless you've been in that situation and felt the shame and embarrassment for yourself.

Mother made sure we always had food to eat and clothes to wear, but she was a victim of the system nonetheless. While she never stooped so low as to accept any form of work that was immoral or illegal, the fact that she had no marketable job skills or career education meant that she had to take whatever other employment she could find in order to keep our family intact.

I have no idea how—or if—my brother and sisters and I would have survived without the added structure that Auntie and Uncle provided at several key times in our childhood. However, it would have been so much easier if there had been a man around the house to provide the father image we so desperately needed and to give Mother a break from the enormous load she carried. We needed a dad to give us a sense of balance and security, to support us emotionally as well as physically. As much as I love and respect my uncle, no man could ever take the place of the father who walked out of my life before I was born.

Looking back, I can only say I owe an enormous debt to my dear mother and auntie. Those two strong women were the biggest influences in my upbringing, and I shudder to think what I would have become without them. Auntie instilled a deep sense of reverence and respect for authority in me. Mother demanded that I treat her with dignity. And they stood together in their determination to keep me out of the gangs regardless of the cost. When the pressure in my home neighborhood became too strong, Mother would ship me to Auntie's home, and vice versa. I learned to love and obey my mother and my aunt. Against seemingly insurmountable odds, I became a good child. And even though I made a number of mistakes growing up in that dangerous South Side environment, I still managed to survive even without a father to guide and correct me.

I can't think of two finer women in the world.

Chapter Four

The Trip to See Dad

Things were going well for me in the twelfth year of my life. I was full of the natural optimism of youth and looking forward to the increasing freedom that comes with the onset of the teen years. Our home life was pleasant and nurturing, and I was doing well in school. And to top it off, my basketball skills were rapidly improving, and I was gaining a reputation as a talented athlete. The only dark shadows looming on the horizon were the challenges of coping with the gangs and the fact that I was missing my father—a lot!

William Harris had not been a member of our family for many years. I desperately needed his strong, fatherly presence in my life and had never understood why he wasn't living with us anymore. I felt a gnawing emptiness inside my heart and craved the love and attention of my father. I would have given anything for one of his hugs or a bit of paternal advice. I used to fantasize about how it would feel to receive a word of encouragement from my dad when I made a difficult basketball shot or did well on a test at school.

So you can imagine the intense excitement I felt the day I learned we were going to see him again. When I came home from school, my sisters were all abuzz in an exceptionally good mood. They could hardly wait to tell me the news.

"Dad called!" they exclaimed. "He wants us to come back to Indianapolis to see him. We're going to leave next week!"

I can't begin to tell you how elated I felt!

The trip to see Dad seemed to me to take an eternity—a happy eternity, to be sure, but an interminable one nonetheless. After we packed our belongings and piled into the car, Dad was all I could think about. I kept imagining what it was going to be like to see him again. What did he look like after all these years? I thought about things we could do together, places we could go, games we could play. I could almost see us going to shoot baskets as father and son.

It was early afternoon when we finally arrived in Indianapolis. Dad was still at work, so we drove to the home of one of our aunts. Everyone was happy to see us. There were hugs all around, and we all pitched in to unload the car. After we caught up on the latest news and small talk, I sat on the floor and turned on the TV, Mom sank into an easy chair, and the girls grabbed the sofa. It felt good to relax; it had been a long trip, and we were tired.

A couple of hours later we heard footsteps coming up the stairs. I jumped off the floor and stood as tall and straight as I could. Adrenaline pounded through my veins as every cell of my body went on full alert. I wanted to make a good impression on Dad!

Mother met him at the door, and the two of them fell into a long embrace. "It sure is good to have you home again!" he enthused. When he released her, Dad turned to my two older sisters. "This is my oldest daughter, Gloria!" he said, beaming as he picked her up and planted a big fat kiss on her lips. "And here is Virginia, my second oldest daughter. Honey, how you have grown!" he exclaimed as he hugged her and swung her around in a big looping circle.

From where I was standing, I could see that my father was tall, dark-skinned, and very handsome. I was so proud of him! He was a strapping, good-looking man, and I knew I would someday grow up just like him.

Nothing in the world could have prepared me for what happened next. After resoundingly welcoming my mother and sisters, Mr. William Harris turned coolly towards me. The absence of warmth and affection chilled me to the depths of my soul. "I remember you," he said casually.

That was it. No handshake. No hug. No pat on the back. No "This must be Michael, my son!" Nothing like "My, what a fine young man he's turning out to be!" No "I'm so proud of my son!" Nothing but a devastating "I remember you."

For one awkward, agonizing minute I stood there, too saddened to move. The loving, affirming father of my fondest dreams had just dismissed me outright, and there was nothing I could do to turn the situation around. To make things worse, I had no idea what I had said or done to merit his disapproval.

Why didn't he like me? Why wasn't my father as excited to see me as he was to see the girls? Why didn't I rate a hug too? Had I let him down in some way? Was he disappointed with the way I looked?

The moment Dad turned his attention back to my mother, I slipped out the door and bolted for the car. I crawled into the back seat and curled up like a baby. When I could see that I hadn't been followed, I cut loose and cried a torrent of tears. My heart was truly broken—my father had rejected me!

I don't know how long I lay there sobbing out all the pain of my life, but it must have been a few hours. Darkness fell, and, knowing I couldn't stay in the car all night, I dried my tears, straightened my shirt, and tried to appear nonchalant as I slunk back inside the house and found my way to the room where I would be sleeping.

A bit later, Mother came in and started rubbing my back. She could tell how unhappy I was. "I know you're hurting, Baby," she said. "There's something I need to tell you. I've been meaning to tell you for a long time. You deserve to know what's going on."

During the next few minutes, Mother told me the sad story I had never suspected, not in my wildest dreams. While she was married to William Harris, she'd had an extramarital affair and had gotten pregnant. Nine months later, when I came on the scene, she and Mr. Harris did their best to make a go of the relationship, but my presence in the home was a constant testimony to her indiscretion. Somehow they managed to hold things together until I was five, but then they separated and went through a bitter divorce.

As Mother finished telling her story, I gradually adjusted to the shock and finally came to realize that Mr. Harris wasn't really my father. Nor, I gradually understood, was he able to assume that role in my life. In a way, it was a relief. He hadn't actually been rejecting me; he'd been reacting against the painful betrayal that had led to the downfall of his marriage to the woman he so obviously loved.

This news left some enormous unsettled questions in my mind: Who *was* my father? What was he like? Did I look like him? Was he an athlete like me? Did we like the same teams? When could I meet him? I needed to know!

For reasons I'll never know this side of heaven, Mother never told me. Each time I dared to ask, she got upset. I don't know if she was ashamed or embarrassed. I don't know if my father was a gangster, a politician, or just some guy she met at work. All I know is she never told me the truth. Every time I tried to broach the subject, Mother would get angry and clam up. She never gave me the slightest clue as to who my father was or why she didn't want me to find out.

The twelfth year of life is crucial to the development of a healthy adult identity. Events that happen during that year—positive or negative—leave an indelible imprint on the developing sense of self. In my case, rejection by the man I thought was my father was harder to take than anything else I've ever had to face in my life. Coupled with the shocking story my mother told me later that evening, it's no wonder I felt so overwhelmingly horrible. The two ugly, soul-stabbing realizations in a few short hours were more than I could handle. Looking back on that traumatic episode, I can't help but wonder if the seeds of despair and alienation that were planted so deep in the soft soil of my heart at that time didn't eventually become the roots of my raging addiction to drugs later in life.

As I grew into adulthood, I finally managed to empathize with the pain and conflict my mother must have felt over the tragic affair that broke up her home. Nevertheless, I still don't understand why she never did reveal the identity of my father.

Mother's final days were filled with severe pain as she battled bravely against cancer of the liver and pancreas. Thanks to the strength I've found in my relationship with the Lord, I was able to bury the hatchet and give her my full love and support. But she carried the secret of my father's identity to her grave.

When we get to heaven, I know my questions will be answered by the same heavenly Father who has walked with me every step of the way. He promised never to leave or forsake me, and He's been keeping that promise every day of my life.

I can't tell you how much I'm looking forward to my next trip to meet my Father. Because of His healing grace, it's going to turn out a whole lot better than the last one.

Chapter Five

Crossing the Racial Divide

The end of my sixth-grade year marked an important transition in my life. Prior to that time, I had lived entirely within the boundaries of the Black communities of Indianapolis and Chicago, but now, with my advancement to seventh grade, I was introduced to the other side of the ethnographic divide.

The decision had been made for me to transfer to Ray School, a predominantly White middle school on the opposite side of the color line. Even though the walk to Ray took only twenty minutes, I discovered a whole new way of life over there. I didn't know what to expect. I had heard many things about White people, but I soon discovered that prejudice cuts both ways. Some of the information I had picked up about the White community proved untrue once I got there and checked things out for myself.

For one thing, even though I was one of only a handful of Blacks at the school, I soon discovered that I was very well liked. My natural charisma and outgoing personality accelerated my acceptance into the mainstream of school society, and before long, I had made a whole new set of friends. I was motivated to make the most of my opportunities and soon decided to get involved in school politics. The leadership qualities God gave me quickly rose to the surface, and within months of transferring to Ray School, I was elected president of the student body.

I had lots of fun that year. When the faculty announced an open invitation for a student talent show, a group of us decided to lip-sync one of our favorite tunes from a popular Motown recording group. In my role as lead singer, I enjoyed the music so much I actually started singing. I didn't think much of my vocal abilities at the time, I just felt like singing along. Little did I realize that God would one day use the talents He had given me to glorify His Son! All I knew then was that I enjoyed being the center of attention at Ray School.

Unfortunately, my newfound popularity and success in the White world didn't shield me from the gangs back home. Walking back over the South Side line every afternoon proved to be a daunting challenge. Instead of getting better, things heated up between the gangs and me. It got to the point where I was miserable all the time. I got tired of running from harassment, getting beaten up, and fighting for survival at every turn. In a very real way, my life was becoming a living enactment of the video games kids play nowadays in which a lone warrior constantly faces a barrage of angry assailants coming at him from every quarter. But unlike those games, the pain and fear were torturously real in my life. Frankly, I didn't know if I would live to adulthood.

The constant pressure began to affect my schoolwork. All I could think about was how to get home each evening and back to school the next morning without getting hurt. I finally told my mother how I was feeling. When I did, she decided to move me back to Auntie's for my eighth-grade year.

Auntie lived in a racially mixed community. About half her neighbors were Black and the other half White. Somehow the two races, which can be so antagonistic to one another in other parts of the country, managed to get along very well. When I moved in, the first thing I noticed—with an enormous sigh of relief—was the absence of gangs. It was just what the doctor ordered for my embattled soul and spirit.

I had always loved to play basketball, but back in the Woodlawn area of the South Side, I hadn't dared to practice openly for fear of a drive-by shooting; they weren't uncommon in the parks and YMCA playgrounds where kids went to play. But in the vicinity of Bennett Middle School, I felt safe enough to stretch my wings and enjoy the game.

At first I felt a little silly for not being very good at basketball for one who was so tall. But that all began to change the day I met Matthew, a nice White boy who lived across the street from Auntie and Uncle. Matthew and I were about the same age and soon became the best of friends. He had a basketball court in his backyard, and we played every spare minute. Matthew was very good at his game—so good, in fact, that he made the team at Mendal High, a Catholic school known for producing some of the top athletes in all of Chicago.

I was determined to learn everything I could about the game. Not only was I tired of being ridiculed for not being very good at the sport, but more than that, I wanted to play because basketball had become my passion. I must have had a God-given talent, because once I got started, I quickly picked up the finer points of the sport, and I excelled.

One day, Matthew invited some of his colleagues from Mendal High to come over and play with us after school. The guy defending me was a big White dude who was kind of slow on his feet. Before long, my finesse at evading his defensive maneuvers began to humiliate him, and the next thing I knew, he was calling me the "N" word and using other racial slurs. I didn't let his harassment bother me; I just stayed focused on the game and scored a lot more points on him. But when he turned physical on me, I responded, and we got into a scuffle.

I will always respect Matthew for what happened next. In an act of courage and strength, he stood up to the bully for me. "Michael is a very good person," he said. "He's my friend and my neighbor. I've been watching you, and I don't appreciate some of the things you're doing, so please leave."

To me, Matthew will always exemplify the power of integrity and conviction. I will never forget the way he handled that potentially explosive situation.

Once I moved into high school, doors seemed to open for me. I had lots more freedom, and the thing I wanted to do the most was to play basketball. My skills increased tremendously my freshman year. Because the other players with my talent and height were mostly seniors who would be graduating at the end of the year, I was soon asked to play on the varsity team. Word soon got around that I was the only freshman on the varsity team, and my reputation took a definite turn for the better. I was ready for the challenge. I had all the skills and ability, and, more than that, my heart was in the game.

You've got to be able to jump if you want to shoot hoops, and I soon learned how to leap far above the rim, catch the ball in midair, and stuff it into the net. That gave me an enormous advantage over the opposing players. Before long, everybody was talking about me. And why not? I was the fourteen-year-old superstar freshman who stood six feet, four inches tall and played with the upperclassmen.

My coaches were very impressed too, and the next thing I knew, they were talking about college scholarships and a possible NBA career. "The sky's the limit!" I heard them saying. "Go for it, Michael! You can play for the Bulls!"

The problem was, without a strong male role model in my life, I had no idea how to hunker down and discipline myself for the long haul. It would have been very helpful to me to have a father who could take me aside, encourage my devotion to the game, and counsel me about the stupid, ego-driven mistakes I was making. I'm sure things would have gone better than they did. Nevertheless, I've known people who grew up in far worse circumstances than mine, yet who disciplined themselves to maximize their opportunities and become successful at whatever they chose to do. Sometimes people take stock of what they don't have and reach their goals by the sheer force of will and determination. But in my case, my lack of discipline became my greatest weakness.

I knew better, but the desire to enhance my image of being the cool, macho jock motivated me to start smoking. Looking back, I can see that smoking is the single stupidest thing a guy who wants to become a star athlete can possibly do. The road to success in any sport is to stay drug-free and healthy. But I wanted to hang with the crowd, and before long, I was helplessly hooked.

Cigarettes are bad enough on their own, but I soon began smoking pot and popping pills, mostly barbiturates, by the handful. The next thing I knew, I was getting into wine and other forms of alcohol. Looking back, it's difficult to say why I started drinking and abusing drugs, but at the time I thought it made me feel good. Besides, many of my friends were experimenting with chemical-induced highs, and it seemed like the thing to do. But it was exactly the wrong thing to do! I thought I was in control of my life. I felt like I was really having fun. It seemed I had found the missing dimension of power and influence I had been seeking for so long. I was sure I could put the drugs down whenever I wanted. I had every confidence in the world that I would never get hooked, but I was dead wrong.

The first thing that began to change was my attitude. I became arrogant and started acting superior to other people. I felt that since I was so well liked, since I played on the varsity team, everyone who passed me in the hall should take notice of me and acknowledge who I was. When that didn't happen, I became irritated and rude.

By the beginning of my sophomore year, things were going from bad to worse. My grades began falling, and I couldn't bring them up. I knew the rules: If my grades slipped below a C average, I would have to leave the team. My coaches grew increasingly alarmed, but instead of confronting me and forcing me to get the help that I needed, they began to pressure my teachers to alter my grades.

But even that didn't work for long. Drugs stole my ambition to apply myself and try to turn things around. I put forth no effort to bring my grades up, and instead of developing the kind of study habits that would have stood me in good stead for the rest of my life, I sank into the quagmire of depression. The more I struggled, the faster I flunked.

In my work today as a Christian recording artist with a ministry that spans the globe, I always encourage young people that if they have a dream, they better fight for it by building the kind of solid, foundational skills necessary to make it come true. I tell them from my own hard experience that the biggest part of laying the groundwork for success is getting a good education. As boring as it sometimes seems, a good education is the base they will stand on for the rest of their lives.

By the time I graduated from high school, I was no longer on the basketball team. Although I was still a very good player with very strong athletic abilities and a passionate love for every aspect of the sport, I had fallen into the trap of believing that talent and dreams are all it takes to succeed. In the attempt to find fulfillment through drugs and booze, I lost sight of the prize and shot myself in the proverbial foot.

Even so, God had planted a desire for something better in my heart, and that desire began to take root in a powerful way. No matter where I looked on the South Side, I couldn't find what I wanted. My friends were all hooked on drugs and booze. To a man, they had all fallen into one pit of despair or another, and I was tired of such a dismal environment. I wanted to move on to something better—to a place where shots weren't fired every night, where folks didn't sit on the porch smoking marijuana. I wanted a place where lawns and flowers grew. I wanted to go to a place where the windows—and the people—weren't always broken.

I'd gotten a taste of the world I wanted while I was staying with Auntie and Uncle, but whenever I went back to Mother's house, the old life was right there, staring me in the face and dragging me down. I was sick and tired of watching lives go down the drain and seeing my friends get sucked in by the violence and despair all around them. I felt driven to find a better way of life. That drive wouldn't let me go until I moved on.

I lived in a miserable state of indecision for a whole year. I found work on the South Side, but my heart was always somewhere else. Auntie had planted a good seed in my heart, and it was starting to bloom. I'll never forget her telling me, "Michael, if you have faith like a grain of mustard seed, you can call out to the mountains to move, and they'll get out of the way."

And even though I hadn't built the solid foundation I needed during my high-school years, God was still working on me. Even though the forces of addiction and destruction were battling against me and pulling me down, they were strongly opposed by the powerful spiritual forces God had inspired my aunt to plant deep within my soul.

One day it all came to a head. I don't remember everything that was going on in my mind and heart that afternoon. The only thing that mattered was the fact that I finally decided I couldn't stand the South Side one more day.

Chapter Six

I Get Out
of Town

There must be a better place to live than Chicago! I said to myself one fateful afternoon. Graffiti covered the walls, trash littered the sidewalk, and it didn't take a rocket scientist to figure out that my surroundings weren't exactly pristine. In fact, they were downright disgusting! I knew it was time to leave, but how?

The next time I went to the mall, I stopped at the U.S. Navy recruiting office and talked with the smart-looking officer on duty. He painted Navy life in glowing, adventurous terms that appealed to every fiber of my being. Not only would joining the Navy get me out of Chicago, but it would provide an unprecedented opportunity for me to see the world and launch a career. The idea seemed tailor-made to my needs.

But did I have the mental discipline to succeed in the precisely organized world of the Navy? After years of barely getting by, could I acquire the diligent study habits it would take to thrive and survive? I gave the issue serious consideration while the recruiting officer continued his discussion of the features, advantages, and benefits of Navy life. By the time he moved in for the close, I had made up my mind. I was going to give it everything I had. I would learn to act, dress, and think like a Navy man.

The next few weeks were times of difficult adjustment for me. The Navy was a racially diverse environment, and for the first time since I was a small boy, I was free of the terrorism of the gangs. I enjoyed getting acquainted with people from so many different cultures and ways of life. My mind began to grasp a whirlwind of exciting possibilities as I traveled around the globe.

One of the most liberating discoveries I made was that most of the world was free of the paralyzing hatred and anger I had known back on the South Side. The more I saw of the positive opportunities of life, the more I realized there was a wonderful world out there just waiting to be explored. And as I saw the squalor and poverty in certain parts of the world, I actually began to appreciate the freedom and opportunity I had taken for granted as an American citizen. I could see that not everyone in this world has the same privileges as we do.

One thing didn't change, however. I brought my social lifestyle with me—I kept smoking pot and drinking beer and wine. And even though I stayed high all night and partied "till the cows came home," as the saying goes, I always managed to check into work like a professional the next day.

The guise worked pretty well. I actually started believing I could fool everyone. In fact, it was years before anyone even suspected that I was abusing drugs and alcohol. But in the back of my mind, I knew I wasn't fooling God. I knew the big, loving heart of Jesus was breaking because of the terrible choices I was making in my life. However, I also always realized that He would never stop loving me in spite of what I was doing to myself. The still, small voice kept insisting that God would never abandon me.

As harmless and innocent as the marijuana I was smoking seemed, it proved to be a gateway for me into a world of powerful, addictive drugs that would eventually overpower and destroy my life. As much as I liked to pretend I was in control, I soon found myself experimenting with hard drugs like cocaine and heroin. I had heard that drugs can kill, but I thought I was stronger than other people. After all, if I could fool Uncle Sam, I was smart enough to stay in control of my own destiny.

Boy, was I wrong!

As I travel around the country today, I find that many young people think the way I did. They think drugs are cool and that they can quit any time they want to. That you have to take a risk if you want to have fun. I tell them to stay away from drugs of all sorts because drugs maim and kill. Then I point to my wife, Amber, in her wheelchair as living proof of what I mean. I encourage them to get to know Jesus Christ and to believe that our Lord and Savior has a plan for their lives that involves purpose and power.

I also remind them that Satan has a plan too—a plan for their destruction and death! It's my prayer that people everywhere will turn to the Lord Jesus Christ and find freedom and fulfillment in life. If you haven't turned your life over to Him, you're missing the best life has to offer. He can take you to higher ground than all the drugs in the world, and His purpose is to give you abundant, everlasting life. It sure beats the stuffing out of the alternative!

When my four years with the Navy came to an end, I had performed very well, and my superiors were happy with my progress. They wanted me to reenlist for another term. After all, they said, I had already advanced to the level of an E-5 second-class petty officer—who knew how high I might climb if I stayed on board?

I was flattered and tempted, but the more I thought about it, the more I realized it was time to move on. The Navy lifestyle had taught me a lot about life, and it had broadened my horizons immensely. But deep inside, I knew it was time to come ashore and plant my roots somewhere else. And so it was that on June 1, 1978, I got off the boat in Port Hueneme, California, and found a job as a civil service worker for the United States government.

It was also in Port Hueneme that I managed to catch the eye of a beautiful young lady at the Bank of America who would become the love of my life.

It didn't take long for me to figure out that I was ready for my next adventure.

Chapter Seven

Island Girl

Remember that beautiful banker I met in Port Hueneme, California? It turns out she came from the Fiji Islands, and her name was Amber Whippy.

I'd been watching Amber a lot. In fact, when I had business there at the bank where she worked—and that was suddenly happening quite often—I studied her every move. I don't know how to explain it other than to say that I was falling in love. It wasn't just her fair skin and radiant smile that drew me in. The way her eyes danced with intelligence and warmth captivated my interest. Every time I left the bank, her beauty haunted me until I could think of another excuse to go there again.

My infatuation with Amber almost got me arrested one afternoon. I had gone to the bank to deposit my paycheck. I was hoping, of course, that she'd be there, and she was. That day she looked more wonderful to me than ever. I was secretly hoping that depositing the check would take all day, but it didn't, of course. And when the transaction was finished, I had no choice but to return to the car.

But rather than just drive away, I sat in my car in the parking lot, enchanted and infatuated. Had she noticed me? Did she know I loved her? How could I hope to capture her affection?

The more I thought about it, the more I knew I couldn't leave without seeing her one more time. So I got out of the car, re-entered the bank, and stood in line again, taking every opportunity to admire her beauty. When I reached the teller, I said that I had decided to withdraw the money I had just deposited.

Once again I finished my business inside the bank and headed back to the car. This time I knew I was smitten—Amber was absolutely the most beautiful woman in the world! My infatuation was attaining critical mass. I had to see her one more time!

When I marched back into the bank for the third time in less than an hour, the security guard became very suspicious. Either I was the most indecisive customer in the world or I was getting ready to rob the bank! He kept a wary eye on me the whole time.

One afternoon, Amber got a beautiful bouquet of white carnations from a mysterious "Mr. J." Unfortunately for me, she had no idea who might have sent them. When I finally did step forward a few weeks later, she smiled as if to say, "Oh, it was you!" Then I mustered up all the courage I could find to ask her out, and Amber shocked me by saying Yes.

By this time, I wanted to know everything about her. But I was afraid she'd turn up her cute little nose and walk away if I appeared too eager, so I took my time and planned my approach. And eventually, little by little, the story began to unfold.

The town where Amber grew up goes by the name of Savu Savu. To find it, just draw a line north from New Zealand and another one west from Samoa until you come to Fiji. Then look for the island of Vanua Levu. Savu Savu is right there. If you see a little grass hut with a thatched roof and lots of little kids running around outside, chances are you're in Amber's neighborhood.

Any way you look at it, the Fiji Islands are about as different from the South Side of Chicago as you can get on this planet. Instead of the world of concrete, gangs, and graffiti where I grew up, Fiji offers a pristine environment of lush tropical forests, beautiful white beaches, and clear blue waters. And compared to what I had known in Chicago, life in Savu Savu was bucolic and relaxed. Islanders bathe in crystal rivers that flow from deep underground springs on the sides of towering volcanic mountains. They snorkel on the reefs and fish in the sea. In fact, every morning before school, Amber's father would awaken the kids at dawn and send them down to the sea to catch their lunch. You might say that's fresh fish!

Amber especially enjoyed holidays. Grandma and Grandpa Jackson, her mother's parents, would pick the children up in their boat after school and transport them to the coconut plantation where they lived on another part of the island—a three-hour journey. The best part of the trip came when Grandpa would blow a large conch shell and porpoises would suddenly appear and follow the boat for nearly a mile. Amber and her siblings loved to watch them swim beside the boat.

Amber's upbringing had provided her with something else that mine lacked: an awareness of the cultural differences in today's pluralistic world. Most of her family members descended from the Fijian branch of the Melanesian people; in fact, some of them were island chiefs and royalty. But one of her ancestors on her father's side was a salty Nantucket whaler by the name of David Whippy.

The story of how Mr. Whippy became the first American consul general in the Fiji Islands is a fascinating tale of adventure and intrigue. As a young man, David Whippy had signed on to serve a whaling ship bound for the islands of the blue Pacific. By the time the boat reached Fiji, he was sick and tired of the strict regimen on board, so he abandoned ship. It couldn't have been easy for a deserter to survive in those days; the Fijis were considered the most dangerous of all the cannibal islands. But with his considerable diplomatic skills, Mr. Whippy not only managed to negotiate his survival but also became a favorite of the island monarch, King Cakobau.

Amber's paternal grandmother came from a chiefly family of the powerful Tuikaba tribe, the same clan as King Cakobau. The interaction of her ancestors with Mr. Whippy would not only change the face of Fijian history forever but also exert a powerful influence over the politics and cross-cultural relations of the entire Pacific Rim to this day.

Mr. Whippy soon adopted the local lifestyle and devoted the rest of his life to advancing the health and welfare of the islanders. He is credited with building the first European-style seagoing vessel in Fiji. Having mastered the intricacies of the local dialect, he found his skills as an interpreter in high demand as a succession of British and American explorers began to call on the islands in the 1840s. When the Fiji Islands were ceded to Great Britain in 1874, Mr. Whippy acted as official interpreter for the ceremonies.

Grandma and Grandpa Jackson instilled their love for God in Amber from an early age. Grandma Jackson was a devout Methodist who conscientiously observed Sunday as the day of rest, while Amber's beloved grandpa was just as enthusiastic about keeping Sabbath on Saturday, in harmony with the teachings of the Seventh-day Adventist Church. Amber thought she was lucky to get two days off each week while her friends got only one.

Amber loved her grandpa; he was a wonderful man. He had helped build the first church in Savu Savu. He loved to gather his grandchildren around him on the veranda every morning and evening while he read them the stories of the Bible for worship.

Fridays, the preparation day for the Sabbath, were always special at Grandma and Grandpa Jackson's place. On that day Grandpa would load the kids into his boat and row them across the river to gather food for the holy day. Their cousins, who lived on a nearby plantation, would always come to help. Once the children had collected enough fruit, Grandpa would let them play. They loved to swim in the river, chew fresh sugar cane, and listen to the birds and animals of the forest.

I learned Amber's story as we dated. I took her to all the best restaurants and did my utmost to let her know I thought she was extremely special. And I tried to impress upon her that I was a wonderful man. We had a fabulous time together, and before long I realized she wasn't enjoying just the wining and dining—she was also enjoying being with me. *This is too good to be true!* I thought to myself.

A month later, I was ready to pop the question. That's right, THE question. The one girls dream about and guys dread like an amputation.

Chapter Eight

The Whole Enchilada

Women love to read about romance. Guys pretend they don't, but I suspect that way down inside, there's a bit of the romantic in most of us. I have to admit I never get tired of telling the story of how Amber and I got together.

Amber had been married once before. She was only eighteen at the time, and she was working for Qantas Airlines at Nadi International Airport on Viti Levu, the largest island in the Fijian chain. As she looks back now, she realizes that God was preparing her for a very special work, but she couldn't have known it then. Her son from that first marriage, a handsome young man named Christopher Louis, played a mighty role in God's plan.

When Amber and her first husband divorced, she felt a sense of responsibility for Chris. California sounded like the land of opportunity. There she could find better employment than she had, and Christopher could get a superior education. Besides, she was disappointed and depressed, and she thought a change of scenery would do them both good.

In her loneliness and grief, Amber began talking to God again—something she had been neglecting to do for the past few years. "I'm sorry, Father," she told Him, "for leaving You out of my life. I know You're not happy with some of the things I've been doing. Please help me."

During those intimate conversations with the Lord, Amber also confided that she felt she couldn't go on living in a world of broken relationships without a stable marriage, especially now that she had a son. She always concluded by asking the Father to send her "someone who will last a lifetime."

That, of course, was the role God was tapping me to play. I needed someone, too—someone with the sensitivity and warmth to value a relationship and cherish me for the person I was becoming, even as I would love and honor her for who she was.

One of the things that makes romance so exciting is the chance it provides to forge something entirely new out of two separate lives; to pick and choose the elements of your own romantic tapestry from the influences of two pasts and two personalities. And if the two parties have even a pinch of creative imagination, the whole process becomes a joyful exploration of the infinite possibilities of life. Was I, for instance, the self-proclaimed Mr. J, a big-time basketball star like Julius Irving? Or was I a Black prince from the African savannah, as I playfully insisted? Amber said I could easily have passed for either one. She said I was gallant and charming regardless of who I really was or where I came from.

I, on the other hand, always felt she was the glamorous one. I was fascinated by her stories of life on Fiji—of growing up in a world of sunny days and moonlit beaches where laughter wafted on the breeze all hours of the day and night. I could only imagine how it must feel to live in such a heavenly environment among people who, just a century earlier, had been cannibals and headhunters. The whole place seemed exotic and enchanting beyond words.

As Amber's and my connections to each other began to deepen, I felt it was important to take her to church. We had a wonderful time; both of us were happy to discover we shared a Christian heritage.

Even though we were falling deeper and deeper in love, however, I didn't feel the time had come for me to share all my secrets with Amber. For one thing, I didn't want her to know that I smoked. Not yet, anyway. For another, I wasn't eager for her to learn that I drank alcohol and smoked marijuana regularly either.

There was one thing I *did* want to communicate to her: that was how very much I loved her. Sometimes a man just knows, and I knew I wanted Amber to be my wife. We hadn't been dating very long when I asked her to marry me. To my great joy, she said "Yes!" And so, on March 3, 1984, I pledged my love and fidelity to Amber Whippy "until death do us part."

Neither of us had the faintest idea how close we would come to a literal fulfillment of the words of our vow. Nor, for that matter, how soon that brush with death would occur.

Chapter Nine

Till Disillusionment Do Us Part

After our beautiful wedding, Amber and I settled down to the difficult job of getting to know each other. Two people may adamantly insist they know everything important about each other. But even though they're very much in love, the masks don't come off until the honeymoon's over. That's when things get real. In fact, experts say the first two years of marriage are usually the hardest. If a couple can survive those years, they stand a pretty good chance of making their marriage last a lifetime.

I did what I could to conceal my smoking and drug use from Amber, but once you're married, it's pointless to try to keep secrets. She was bitterly disappointed in me. Nothing in her background or upbringing had prepared her to accept pot smoking and doing drugs as healthy or normal. Amber was so angry the day she discovered that I couldn't face going to church without smoking a joint that she held an impromptu prayer meeting to discuss it with the Lord.

Her prayer on that occasion certainly wasn't the longest in history, nor even the most eloquent or profound. But it came straight from the heart, and that always counts with God. Short, to the point, and very intense, it served as a cogent expression of her deep sense of disappointment. After everything she had endured in her first marriage, after her repeated pleas for God to send her a stable Christian husband who would help her grow in grace and who would serve as an exemplary masculine role model for Chris, she felt let down and ripped off. She concluded her complaint by reminding God that "this is not what I prayed for!"

Instead of experiencing wedded bliss, Amber and I gradually drifted onto the reefs of disaster. Marriage is seldom easy. The task of blending two different personalities into a viable relationship, of navigating the perennial challenges of who's in charge and how and where to draw the lines requires a lot of time, understanding, and maturity. It's tough enough when both partners are clean and sober. It can be nearly impossible when one of the partners is battling several powerful addictions at once—especially, as in our case, when that partner refuses to acknowledge he has a problem.

As I fell further and further into the grip of my addictions, Amber occasionally joined me in having a glass of champagne or smoking a joint. But thanks to a healthy dose of common sense buttressed by her strong, choleric temperament, she quickly realized she was encouraging my destructive behavior and stopped participating in it. However, without the tactfulness, wisdom, and skill that can come only from a solid and living connection with the Lord, her efforts to help led only to greater disillusionment and distance between us. We argued constantly, and both of us felt increasingly miserable. We were very inexperienced, and the suffering we inflicted on each other was intense.

By the time Amber finally realized the crisis in our marriage was beyond her ability to handle, it was almost too late. I say almost because "with God, all things are possible." Fortunately for us, she turned to God for help.

Often when people first surrender a problem to God, they believe He'll iron out all the difficulties quickly and painlessly. God *can* operate like that, and I am convinced that He *does* work in that manner when He sees that's what we need. But sometimes we humans are so stubborn and our habits are so deeply entrenched that God chooses to take the long way around. Fortunately for us, He never abandons us, even though we sometimes think that's exactly what's going on.

In our case, God's first assignment was to get me to admit that I was hooked. Because of Amber's strong personality, I found it easy to blame my problems on her. *If only my wife weren't so bossy and controlling,* I would say to myself, *things wouldn't get to me, and I could handle the stresses of life on my own.* Of course, this excuse enabled me to avoid taking responsibility; it excused me from admitting that I needed to change. The most deluded people in the world are those who blame everyone else for their own failure to live the way they know they should.

For her part, Amber didn't know more than the barest essentials of the Christian faith. Like many people who pray and go to church, she hadn't even begun to comprehend the essence of the gospel. But that didn't prevent God from answering her prayers. If God waited for people to become experts at living the Christian life before He would reach out to save them, no one would get to first base. Instead, He meets us where we are and does the heavy lifting for us.

A little song Amber had learned in childhood became especially meaningful to her as she became more and more acutely aware that we were heading in the wrong direction fast. "Into my heart; into my heart; come into my heart, Lord Jesus," she would sing over and over. "Come in today, come in to stay; come into my heart, Lord Jesus."

Had Amber known how God was planning to answer that prayer, she undoubtedly would have stopped praying altogether. Since she didn't know, she kept singing it to invite Christ into her heart at all hours of the day and night.

The day of reckoning was just around the corner.

Chapter Ten

Friday Morning Storm Warning

Every year in the United States, more people die in car wrecks than in all the wars this country ever fought put together. More than in the two world wars and Korea and Vietnam and the two Gulf wars plus the Civil War and the American Revolution. Add up all the casualties from every conflict our nation has ever waged, and automobile accidents outweigh the grisly total by a wide margin.

That fact boggles the mind. But let me assure you, it takes on an entirely different significance when someone you love almost dies that way.

The day Amber and I nearly died started out like any typical Friday morning—for me, anyway. I didn't notice anything unusual, but when the alarm went off at 6:30 A.M., Amber didn't hop out of bed as she normally did. Trapped at the intersection of dreams and reality, she suddenly came to realize she couldn't find the power to move. The experience disturbed her immensely.

"I felt paralyzed," she says. "It was like I was caught within a dream or a vision, yet I knew I was at least partially conscious and awake. It was a very strange feeling!"

She still couldn't explain it a few minutes later when she did manage to get out of bed. Why was she feeling so reluctant to face the day? Had she received some kind of premonition or warning? The bizarre incident haunted her all day long. A nameless dread hung over her spirit like a dark cloud that she could neither see nor deny. When she mentioned the incident to one of her girlfriends at work that day, her friend advised her not to talk about it. "It might come true," she said. And even though Amber's never been particularly superstitious, she still couldn't shake the horrifying sense of foreboding that clung to her all day long.

I felt that worrying about intangibles made no sense. My training in the military had given me the confidence to go full speed ahead. I wasn't about to let an irrational fear ruin our plans for an exciting weekend in Las Vegas.

Amber and I had been planning the trip ever since my mother had called to say she was going there. "Why don't you and Amber come out there and join me for the weekend?" she'd said.

It seemed like a good idea. Mother hadn't been able to make it to our wedding, so she and Amber had never met. Her trip to Las Vegas seemed like the perfect opportunity for them to get acquainted and for the three of us to have a good time.

I've been speaking English all my life, but I don't think I'll ever understand all the complexities of our language. Who, for instance, decided that a marijuana cigarette should be called a "joint"—or "pot," for that matter? Maybe I'll never know. All I do know is that while Amber was fixing supper that fateful evening, I felt a joint would help me relax before the long drive across the desert. So I lit one and smoked it.

Amber wasn't exactly happy about that. "You shouldn't be getting high," she scolded. "You're going to be driving!"

I told her not to worry. "Pot helps me relax," I insisted. Then I smoked another joint for good measure. And by the time we left, not only had I eaten a delicious supper and smoked two joints, but I had also downed a couple beers to put me in the mood to face the road.

Is there any reason in the world why a grown man would think that consuming drugs and alcohol would improve his chances of successfully navigating a long, hard drive in the middle of the night? Of course not! That was only my addiction talking, but I was in no condition to resist its twisted logic.

The same blind luck that had gotten me through four years in the military without any visible symptoms of alcoholism and drug abuse got me down the road the first two hours of that night without the slightest indication of trouble. Chalk it up to a tough constitution or a good set of nerves, but I did just fine. Amber mentioned her bizarre premonition a time or two, but I brushed it aside and told her everything was going just fine.

We stopped for coffee at a cafe somewhere along Interstate 15. When we got back in the car, Amber said she felt like taking a nap. She climbed in the back seat and lay down, and I guided the car back out to the highway and settled in for the long haul.

By the time I got us up to speed, Amber was dozing off to her last peaceful dream for many a moon. The seatbelt lay unbuckled beside her. Her premonition of paralysis was about to come true.

Chapter Eleven

Crashing Into Eternity

Late at night the road can play tricks on a driver's mind. The experts call it "highway hypnosis," but whatever you call it, it's often the shortest distance between nodding off to sleep at the wheel and an appointment at the mortuary.

Somewhere around two in the morning on August 22, 1987, I lost control of our car, a 1987 Ford Escort. I have no idea how fast I was driving at the time, but when the car hit the guardrail, we soared into the air at a very high speed.

People routinely drive a lot faster than they should on the monotonous uphill section of I-15 that links Barstow, California, and Las Vegas, Nevada. For one thing, that stretch of road is a wide, well-maintained ribbon of highway designed to accommodate a large volume of high-speed traffic. For another, the cops there have the reputation of looking the other way. Whether they actually do or not, I can't say. However, the Nevada gaming industry certainly benefits from having a high-velocity freeway that makes their desert oasis easily accessible to the teeming population centers of Southern California.

Whatever the reasons, people routinely drive in excess of eighty, ninety, even one hundred miles per hour on that road. As a result, over the years thousands of people, among them comedian Sam Kinison, have met the undertaker on I-15.

With so much booze and drugs lacing my veins that fateful night, it's a wonder I managed to keep our car on the road as long as I did. Suddenly, though, I realized that we were about to ram headfirst into a guardrail.

The heart-piercing blast of adrenaline that shocked my senses back to reality came half a second too late to avert the biggest tragedy of our lives. There wasn't time to turn the wheel or hit the brakes. I couldn't even scream to Amber to duck behind the seat. In a flash of blinding clarity I realized that she and I were about to die and there was nothing I could do about it.

Worst of all, I had absolutely no doubt that I wasn't ready to appear before the judgment bar of God. My sins weren't forgiven. I hadn't been reborn or transformed or set free. That wasn't true of Amber; she knew God and talked to Him often. But I'd been living like the devil, and now I was racing at warp speed into the jaws of eternal condemnation.

Amber says the last thing she remembers from the accident was the look on my face that she glimpsed on her journey from the back seat to the windshield. Then her head snapped backwards with a loud, sickening sound as she shattered the glass and flew off into space.

Chapter Twelve

A Warm Wind on a Cold Desert Night

Shadows loom menacing and strange on the Mojave Desert at night.

This vast expanse of wilderness, which stretches north from the Mexican border into portions of Arizona, California, and Nevada, is *terra incognito* to the thousands of travelers who race through it on their way to the shrines of instant fortune on the Las Vegas strip. Despite the fact that the Mojave is actually a place of serene beauty under the right circumstances, it looks a lot like the badlands of Hades when you suddenly realize that you've probably killed your wife because you stubbornly insisted—against her protests and your own better judgment—on driving several hundred miles in the middle of the night in an intoxicated condition.

After our car careened through the guardrail and launched into space, it took me a while to wake up from the horrendous impact and get my bearings. When I finally did, the insanity of the macho boast I had made a few hours earlier rose up to mock me in relentless waves of shame and remorse. *"Doesn't bother me,"* I heard myself bragging to Amber only hours earlier. *"I've been smoking pot for years. Doesn't impair my judgment at all. Has the opposite effect. Calms my nerves and helps me relax. Puts me in the right mood to face the road."*

When I came to on that desert floor, I began frantically yelling and searching for Amber. The place where we crashed through the rail was only a hundred feet or so away, but in my inebriated confusion and the darkness, it seemed like a million miles.

"Amber!" I cried over and over. "Can you hear me, Amber? Where are you?"

I've heard some beautiful music in my life, but nothing else ever sounded half as good to me as the faint sound I heard a moment later. It was the faint, breathless response of Amber's whispered voice against the cold silence of the desert. "I'm over here," she replied.

By the time I got to her side, Amber had awakened enough to realize that she was in a world of pain. "I'm badly hurt," she whispered. "You'd better go for help."

As I scrambled up the little hill beside the ravine where Amber lay, she was suddenly wrenched with a jabbing pain that surged through her body in tremors of jagged intensity and fear. When people think they're close to dying, they console themselves by remembering words of encouragement from whatever sources come to mind. In Amber's case, it was bits of Scripture she had memorized as a tiny child in Fiji.

"We come into this world with nothing," she muttered to herself, "and here I am about to leave in the same way." Then she remembered God's promise, "I will never leave you nor forsake you."

Not even at a time like this? she wanted to know.

"Especially not at a time like this," came the gentle reply.

That promise from God was all Amber had to hold on to as she wafted in and out of consciousness. Waves of suffering wracked her body as nerves fired raw, synaptic warnings to her overloaded brain. As she was recovering from one particularly overwhelming jolt of pain, the story of a dying criminal flashed across two thousand years of history into the theater of her mind. *Wow!* she thought. *The thief on the cross! So long as I'm breathing, I still have a chance at everlasting life!*

She dimly remembered reading somewhere in the Bible that if we cry out to the Lord, He will hear us. "Lord Jesus," she shouted on the cold morning air, "forgive my sins! Remember me when You come into Your kingdom!"

When life trembles in the balance, there is a precious clarity, an inexplicable assurance for those who put their faith in Christ. As Amber considered the fragile nature of her own existence, she suddenly realized the wonderful reality that nothing in all the world is half as important as the certainty that one's sins are forgiven and one's eternal life is secure.

In a moment of penetrating insight, she could see that her life had been heading in the wrong direction. "I began to realize what's really important," she told me. "It's not about property or possessions. What really matters is knowing Jesus Christ and having a personal relationship with Him."

None of that made any sense to me when Amber said it that night. It sounded delusional and insubstantial. Nevertheless, her words would haunt me in the weeks and months ahead.

The Holy Spirit kept reminding Amber of stories Grandpa Jackson had told her when she was a girl. Verse after verse of powerful Bible promises kept coming to comfort and console her. "I realized then," she says, "how very important it is to memorize the promises of God."

One passage in particular, the sweet words of God in Jeremiah 29:11-13, brought a peaceful calm to her turbulent soul. "I know the thoughts that I think toward you," she heard the Lord saying to her that night. "Thoughts of peace, and not of evil.... Then shall ye call upon me, and ye shall go and pray unto me, and I will hearken unto you. And ye shall seek me, and find me, when ye shall search for me with all your heart" (KJV).

With these words ringing in her heart, Amber dozed off to sleep for a while. The next thing she knew, I was hovering over her.

"Honey," I said with an edge of despair in my voice, "no one wants to stop to help! They just keep on driving by." I put my head on her chest and started to cry.

My tears bothered Amber more than her pain. What could she do to motivate me to get back out there and keep trying to stop traffic until someone actually came to our aid? Would humor work? She decided to give it a try.

"Michael," she said, "I want you to go out there and stand in the middle of traffic even if you get killed!"

That made me laugh. I rose to my feet and tucked my shirt into my pants.

"OK, Baby," I replied. "I'll go back out and try again."

This time I ran back up the hill and out into the middle of the highway. It must have seemed like a nightmare to the cars speeding past on both sides. There I was, a tall black man with a wild expression on his face, waving my arms and yelling like a madman. Cars swerved left and right, but nobody stopped to help.

Just when I was ready to give up in despair, a man suddenly appeared on the shoulder of the road. He was carrying a flashlight and coming toward me. "What's the matter?" he shouted. "I was standing in my living room when I heard your call for help."

I was amazed. We were in the middle of nowhere, and here was this man offering to help. I hadn't seen any houses for miles. Why was he awake at two in the morning, and what was he doing in his living room at that time of day? For that matter, how could he possibly have heard my calls for help above the din of the traffic?

"We had an accident," I told him. "My wife's hurt really bad."

"I'll call an ambulance," the man said. A moment later, he disappeared into the darkness.

By the time the ambulance finally arrived, it was seven-thirty in the morning. Amber had been lying immobilized on the desert floor for five and a half hours.

I had the presence of mind that night to ask the ambulance driver for the exact location of our accident. Several years later, Amber and I returned to the scene to find the stranger who had saved her life. We wanted to thank him and to ask a few questions.

Thanks to the ambulance driver's directions, we were able to find the spot where we had veered off the road and smashed into the rail. We even found the smashed rail that identified the exact point of impact. But although we searched for hours, there wasn't a house anywhere in sight, and we never did find our mysterious helper.

Are angels awake at two in the morning? You'd have a hard time convincing Amber and me to the contrary!

Chapter Thirteen

The Long Journey Home

Thanks to the doctors, nurses, and other emergency personnel at Valley Hospital Medical Center in Las Vegas, Amber got excellent treatment. They sedated her so heavily that she hardly felt the pain most of those first few days after the accident.

Every time she came to, she would think the whole thing had been nothing but a horrifying nightmare and that she would soon be walking again and living her life as carefree as before. But as the days wore on, she came to realize that nothing would ever be the same again. Not only would she never walk again, but thanks to extensive paralysis in her arms, back, and legs, she would never be able to do most of the things she had taken for granted most of her life. I can't even imagine how depressing that must have been.

I was dealing with plenty of issues of my own. Never before in all my life had I done anything that left me feeling so oppressed and guilt-ridden. No matter where I turned, I found no relief day or night from the wicked fangs of self-condemnation and despair. *"Look what you've done to your wife!"* the relentless voice inside my head would accuse.

The day after Amber arrived at the hospital, she received a huge flower arrangement from the staff at American Commercial Bank, where she worked. It cheered her considerably to realize they were thinking about her. The card they sent said, "If it weren't for the rain, the flowers wouldn't bloom." It also contained a verse of Scripture that—by coincidence?— was the very same text she had read the morning before we left on our trip: "Weeping may endure for a night, but joy comes in the morning" (Psalm 30:5, NKJV).

Amber took comfort from the verses that precede that comforting text as well:

> O LORD my God, I cried out to You, and You have healed me. O LORD, You brought my soul up from the grave; You have kept me alive, that I should not go down to the pit. Sing praise to the LORD, you saints of His. And give thanks at the remembrance of His holy name (verses 2-4).

Amber took that to be an indication from God that things were going to improve for her. I didn't know what to think of it. My depression was darker than the sky had been that awful morning in the desert. At every opportunity I slipped away to score some drugs to ease the pain.

The only way Amber managed to cope with her emotional pain was to listen to songs she had learned as a little girl in Fiji. Songs like "What a Friend We Have in Jesus," "I Must Tell Jesus," and "The Old Rugged Cross" wafted through the chambers of her soul, bringing comfort and temporary relief.

She also thought about her family a lot. She would picture that famous painting of Jesus holding the children on His lap and, in her imagination, substitute Kandace, Chris, her grandchildren, and other family members for the children in the picture.

As the reality of her condition set in, Amber could not find comfort in watching television or listening to secular music. Instead, she withdrew inside the corridors of her mind to scenes of the resurrection morning, when she would exchange her tortured frame for a brand-new, perfectly mobile, utterly glorious, immortal body.

My brokenness manifested itself in a different way. *Why did she have to suffer?* I asked myself a thousand times a day. *It should have been me.*

As questions raged and answers did not come, I found myself drinking and doing drugs almost all the time. I knew I should have stayed by Amber's side at the hospital, but I couldn't stand to see her suffer.

After a week in the hospital, Amber's "wonderful employer," as she called the people of the American Commercial Bank, sent a small jet to

Las Vegas to pick us up and bring us back home. When we landed in Ventura County, she was transported to Saint John's Hospital in Oxnard, where the rehab process began in earnest.

Amber's mom and sister Ida flew in from Fiji and did everything they could to keep her spirits up. Looking back on the situation now, Amber says she doesn't know what she would have done without the two of them. "They were like angels to me!" she remembers. "My mom acted as my physical therapist and Ida kept me from wallowing in self-pity. Just seeing them every day reinforced my will to live."

Recovery from a devastating accident takes a lot of time and patience. Amber's head was fitted with a "halo," which was fastened to her skull with four screws and was attached to a harness that reached clear to her waist. The idea was to immobilize her upper body so her spine could fuse itself back together. But while the disks, nerves, muscles, and tendons of her back were trying to find their way to wholeness again, Amber was completely unable to move. That immobility—so vital to the healing of her spine—left her vulnerable to pressure sores and dermal ulcers. To prevent them, the hospital staff would come to her room every hour and rotate her in the bed.

Every day, the hospital's physical and occupational therapists came to help Amber rehabilitate her muscles. Her assignment consisted in playing with blocks like children often do. But since Amber grew up in the Fiji Islands where kids play with coconuts and fishing nets, this was a totally new experience for her.

This should be child's play, she thought to herself. *All I have to do is pick up the blocks and stack them on top of each other.* To her dismay, however, she found that the task was almost impossible to accomplish in her weakened condition. The effort left her feeling exhausted in every sense of the word. "I felt physically and emotionally drained after each session," she recalls. "Despite the excellent care I was receiving at the hospital, I began to feel more and more depressed."

An accident like the one we endured takes an enormous toll on the spirit as well as the body. For Amber, that meant coming face to face with the dreadful reality that she would never walk again. Here she was, a vibrant young woman who had gone jogging every morning to keep herself in excellent shape. Now she was facing the awful reality that she would be confined to a wheelchair and, to some degree, would be dependent on people for the rest of her life. People who are suddenly thrust into that condition need time to grieve the loss of their familiar body, customary mobility, and everyday routine. Those who haven't lived through a life-altering experience like that can't possibly imagine how devastating it is to every dimension of one's existence.

Back on my own home turf, I found it harder than ever to stay focused on work. On the outside, I projected the image of being a strong, macho warrior, but on the inside, I was barely hanging on to the last shreds of dignity and respectability I could find. I found it horrible to have to answer the question "How's Amber?" all the time. But without her influence in my life, I knew things could only go from bad to worse for me. I couldn't find the will to turn myself around, so I let myself go.

I had no idea how far I would sink before I finally hit rock bottom.

Chapter Fourteen

A Sad Farewell

On the way to physical therapy one day, Amber met a young man who had been hit by a car as he walked beside the road. He was only eighteen at the time of the accident, and now, three years later, he was getting ready to celebrate his twenty-first birthday with his biggest fan and supporter, his grandmother.

Each time his grandmother came to visit, she would put her arms around him, run her hands through his hair, and talk to him. Watching their interaction brought tears to Amber's eyes, and the story of how the young man came to accept his adversity became a source of comfort to her.

"It helped me realize I wasn't the only one to suffer misfortune," she remembers. "He had been an active, able-bodied young man—a lifeguard, actually—with his whole life ahead of him. But when I met him, his head was strapped to the back of the chair to keep it from flopping around, and all his dreams had come to a tragic end. He had no control over any of his movements, and he was drooling at the mouth. 'Lord,' I prayed, 'I've had forty-one good years of life, and this poor child has had only eighteen. Who am I to complain?' Of course that didn't stop me from mourning my own tragic loss, but it did help me look outside myself, and that was a blessing in its own right."

Amber will never forget the day the young man's father wheeled him into her room with a hibiscus flower in his hand. "I have no idea where he got it," she says, "but his dad just seemed to know he wanted to give it to me. I was so pleased that he wanted to express his friendship and appreciation to me in that way."

Despite her new realization that others were suffering, too, Amber still had to face some daunting challenges of her own. Something one of the rehab counselors told her struck her with the force of a hurricane. "You know," the counselor confided in a matter-of-fact tone, "the marriages of severe accident victims almost never survive. There are too many difficult adjustments. Most of the time, the uninjured partner just leaves. You'll need to start preparing yourself for that."

Amber had already noticed that my visits to the hospital were becoming fewer and farther between. She expected me to visit her every day, but by the time I got off work, the last thing I wanted was another depressing reminder that my arrogance and weakness had ruined her life and destroyed her world. It was a lot easier for me to excuse myself and find something else to do especially when that something else involved drugs and alcohol. Of course, that did nothing to hasten my mental or psychological healing. In fact, it was the worst thing I could do.

Even so, Amber would station her wheelchair in front of a window every evening so she could watch the front entrance to see if I was coming up the walk. But as it became increasingly apparent that I wasn't coming to see her anymore, she began to get seriously suspicious.

"Anxious thoughts crowded my mind," she remembers. "Michael is a very good-looking man. His six-foot-seven-inch frame, warm smile, and courtly manners always made him a favorite, especially in his younger days. Girls were always flirting with him, and, being the man of the world that he was, he was always flirting back. Knowing that didn't exactly calm my insecurities. In fact, I knew it would be all too easy for him to just go with the flow, find someone new, and forget about me."

In reality, it wasn't that simple. I loved Amber very much. But the load of guilt and self-condemnation I was carrying was more than I could bear—especially without her wisdom to help me put things in perspective. I needed Amber to help me be strong enough to survive, but seeing her in such a mangled condition—and blaming myself for it—only added to the pain, shame, and self-hatred I was feeling all the time.

Amber took note of the not-so-subtle changes in my behavior. One day I showed up at her rehab session dressed in leather pants and a cut-off T-shirt. She had never seen me dress like that before. A few minutes later I fell asleep for no apparent reason. Amber put two and two together and came to the conclusion that I'd been doing cocaine by intravenous injection. She was right.

Five months after the devastating accident, Amber was released from the hospital. I brought her home and promised to do my best to care for her. I did, too—at least at first. But I soon discovered that it was much harder than I had imagined. She was completely dependent on me. I had to wash her, feed her, bathe her, and help her with all the activities of daily life. I even had to brush her teeth. There was practically nothing she could do for herself.

We did OK for the first few days, but after it became apparent that things weren't going to improve, we started getting on each other's nerves. It would have been hard enough on anyone, but my raging substance-abuse problem compounded the difficulty. Communication broke down, we got into terrible arguments, and our home life quickly became a living hell. Amber realized our marriage was in serious trouble the day I asked her for money to buy drugs.

Pain and depression lead people to act in unpredictable ways. Some folks respond to protracted difficulties by turning to God. Others become so preoccupied with their own suffering that they choose to blame God and run far away from Him. In our case, I hadn't been involved in a healthy relationship with God before the accident, and Amber, who had managed to survive only because of the miraculous grace and comfort of God, gradually drifted away from Him. But as she was forced to face the fact that our marriage was rapidly falling apart, she began to sense again how desperately she needed the strength the Lord could supply from the resourses of His grace.

Amber turned to the book *What Happens When Women Pray* by Evelyn Christenson. As she read, she found her attitude changing and her thinking becoming clearer and more objective. She realized she had a difficult choice to make: She could either stay in the custody and care of a man with an ever-worsening drug addiction and perhaps face a painful and lingering death, or she could go back home to Fiji and live with her family. She knew they would give her the best of care, but she hated the thought of letting me go, especially in my desperate condition.

The more she prayed about it, the more clearly she realized that she would have to leave me to save her life. She didn't tell me she was leaving forever, and I was too blind to read the handwriting on the wall. But the day I drove her to Los Angeles International Airport, Amber knew she was leaving me for good. Even though her heart was breaking, she maintained her composure as we bid farewell. "Michael," she said as she hugged me goodbye, "I'm going to pray for you, and you will be a changed man."

Chapter Fifteen

Amber's Season of the Witch

Back home in Fiji, Amber's family treated her with kindness and love. They gladly tended her every need and gave her the consistent attention that my involvement with drugs had made it impossible for me to provide. But they wanted to give her something more: They longed for her to be completely healed of all her broken bones and paralysis. And so, because of their great love for her, they called for the only healer they truly trusted: a witch by the name of Alumita.

People who live in Western cultures have a very limited understanding of the role of witchcraft and animism in the Third World. Basically stated, primitive folk religions center on the belief that everything in the world is inhabited by one or more good or evil spirits and that illness and misfortune can be corrected only by acts of sacrifice or penance designed to appease the spirits and persuade the evil ones to vacate the body of the sufferer.

The Bible, of course, warns us to have nothing to do with such beliefs and practices. It cautions that these spirits are actually fallen angels known as demons. It says that they are very dangerous and deceptive and that the only safe policy is to trust in the Lord and have nothing to do with these ambassadors from the kingdom of darkness.

Nevertheless, many of the people of the Fiji Islands cling tenaciously to the old ways. Belief in the healing power of witches and other healers with magic powers has been an integral part of their culture for thousands of years. The members of Amber's family were no exception. Alumita had a well-established reputation in the family. For several decades they had called upon her to deal with a host of illnesses and problems. Everyone placed a great deal of trust in her—everyone, that is, except Amber.

An example of the power that witchcraft and ancestral spiritism hold over the population of Fiji can be found in a healing Alumita prescribed for Amber's sister Wilma. During a trance, Alumita told Amber's family that Wilma had an evil spirit living inside her and there were only two ways they could exorcize it. She could either allow herself to be lowered into a smelly pit toilet and eat a meal there in hopes of grossing out the evil spirit and so persuading it to vacate her body. Or she would have to permit herself to be tied up in the ocean in water up to her chest. Not surprisingly, Wilma chose the water cure.

At eleven o'clock on the night before the cure, Alumita channeled her spirit grandfather and told him Wilma was ready. The next day, Wilma, who was eight months pregnant, along with her husband, Timoci; her mother-in-law; and two other women from the village, went down to the beach. No one was supposed to talk to her, but that didn't stop Timoci from sidling up to her and telling her, under his breath, to be brave. He felt an ominous foreboding that something terrible was about to happen to her and the baby.

By the time they finally got to the beach, it was getting dark. Because of Wilma's pregnancy, they elected to tie her to a coconut tree rather than to submerge her in the ocean. When they had tied her to the tree, they scrambled up the hill where Alumita had told them to wait. "Do not look at her," Alumita had warned, "or something terrible will happen."

Wilma tried to be brave, but she was terrified. The night was pitch black, and she couldn't stop trembling. She wanted to run away, but her legs were tied and she was too frightened to cry out for help. Suddenly, she felt an eerie presence standing beside her. She tried to scream, but nothing came out of her throat. As hermit crabs scampered across her toes, Wilma began to pray more desperately than she ever had before.

As she looked out towards the reef, she saw a light moving over the water so fast that her heart nearly leaped from her chest. She knew in a moment that it was the dreaded Fijian spirit Dau Cina, "the one who shines his light." She was terrified that he was coming to devour her and her unborn child.

By the time the prescribed forty-five minutes of treatment was over and Timoci and the others came down the hill to untie Wilma, she was crying so violently that Timoci feared she would give birth right there on the beach. But to everyone's amazement, she didn't. When they finally got home that night, Alumita told everyone that the spirit of one of Wilma's deceased ancestors had protected her and the baby from evil down on the beach. Since Wilma and her family knew nothing of the scriptural teaching about death—namely, that "the dead know not anything"—they were entirely at the mercy of these doctrines of demons.

When Amber listened to Wilma's story, she made up her mind to tell the Lord, "My faith is in You. If I have to choose between being healed through witchcraft or never walking again so long as I live, I'd rather not walk. I choose to follow You."

Although Amber had made up her mind to resist the power of spiritualism, her family still believed Alumita could heal her. So every night at seven-thirty, they would bring the witch into Amber's bedroom to pray over her, and every morning, they would repeat the ritual. And at Alumita's insistence, they discarded all of Amber's medications.

As a result, Amber went into deep pain and shock. "I hallucinated for three weeks," she remembers. "I couldn't recall where I was; I had no recollection whatsoever of the accident. I thought I was going blind or insane. Alumita would give me tea to drink made from the bark of some local trees. Then she would call on the spirits and hold long conversations with them in my bedroom."

Because Alumita mixed a few Christian practices, such as prayer, with her bizarre animistic rituals, Amber's family was deceived into believing that everything she did came from the power of God. But not Amber! "At night I heard terrifying noises right outside my window," she recalls. "It sounded like people were being murdered right there on the spot. I was horrified! But nothing could shake my faith in Jesus. Despite those uncanny, satanic noises, I clung to my faith and prayed desperately to God."

Because of her sister's experience and the stern warning of the Bible against dabbling in occult phenomena, Amber resolutely determined not to give in and put her trust in the power of the witch and her spirits. A few days later, Alumita resigned from the case. She told

Amber's mom, "Your daughter can't be healed because she doesn't believe in what I'm doing."

"I felt an enormous sense of relief," Amber says. "I had made up my mind to be faithful to God no matter what the outcome would be. I would rather be crippled for the rest of my life than surrender my will to the power of Satan."

It has proved to be one of the wisest decisions Amber ever made.

Garden Where the Trade Winds Blow

It was Amber's sister Ida who actually brought her back from the brink of destruction. By the time the family finally gave up on witchcraft, Ida realized something had to be done to save Amber's life.

"Amber and I were brought up in a very loving and close family," Ida says. "We were poor in material things, but had lots of love from our mum and dad." She reflects on the nature of her relationship with Amber and then goes on. "She is older than I am, and as we were growing up, I always looked to her for support and guidance. Wherever Amber went, I would follow. Even when she got married and then later moved to the U.S.A., I would visit her as often as I could."

So close was the connection between the two sisters that on the morning of our accident, Ida was awakened from sleep with Amber on her mind. "All I could think of was Amber," she recalls.

Later that morning, Ida called our home. Of course, we weren't there, but she spoke to Robert, a friend of Amber's son, Chris. Robert didn't say a word about the accident; it wasn't until a few hours later that Chris called and told her what had happened. "When I heard about the accident all I could say was, 'Dear Lord, don't let her be handicapped!' " Ida remembers. "All kinds of terrible pictures were going through my mind."

Ida and Amber's mother flew to the U.S.A. and came to the hospital. When they saw Amber face to face, they could hardly conceal their shock. "I told mum that we were going to be strong and put on a brave face for Amber's sake," Ida remembers. "Mum was strong, but I broke down and couldn't face Amber. She had always been so full of life. To see her lying there with all kinds of stuff screwed to her head and chest and all kinds of machines by her bed was just too much for me."

Even so, Ida got over her initial reaction and gradually found a way to help Amber get her mind off her troubles. "Her whole room was full of flowers, cards, and teddy bears," Ida notes. "I can remember one particular day when she wanted to know who all the cards were from. We did a lot of laughing and crying that day. I told her I didn't want to read another sad card for the rest of my life! She thought it was funny that I would start crying whenever I came to the sad part."

Ida's responsibilities to her own family dictated that she could not remain with Amber at the hospital as long as she wanted, so she reluctantly returned to Fiji. Their mother, however, stayed with Amber for the next six months before returning to the islands. "I don't know what I would have done without her support," Amber acknowledges. "Her presence meant the world to me in those dark days."

When Amber flew home to Fiji, Ida was shocked again as she realized her sister would never be the same. "It was in March 1988," she remembers. "Amber had decided to call it quits on her marriage to Michael. I remember that we hired a mini-bus and drove from Suva to Nadi just as her flight arrived. I couldn't believe my eyes; she had lost so much weight, and her body looked dried up, like parchment. There was something in her eyes that just didn't look normal. She was so weak they had to strap her into her wheelchair. My husband, Ben, said Amber's eyes had the look of death."

Because she had been through so many drastic, life-shattering upheavals in the past few months, Amber had stopped eating by the time she got to Fiji. The stresses of her life had reached unmanageable proportions, and she was running out of the energy and will to survive. First, the accident had brought her active life to a painful halt. Then our marriage had fallen apart as I plunged further and further into the insanity of addiction. After that, the witchcraft "cure" had nearly driven her into the jaws of death. Ida knew something had to be done soon if she didn't want to attend Amber's funeral. So she insisted that Amber move in with her family until she recovered.

As Amber recalls it, Ida's tender loving care was the best therapy in the world. "Every day after my bath," Amber remembers, "Ida and Emele—one of Ida's housekeepers—would massage me from head to toe. It took about an hour, and they did it again every evening before bedtime. It worked wonders for my circulation."

But Ida's loving ministrations didn't end there. Every morning, after Amber's bath and massage, she was wheeled into the garden, where she was offered fresh papaya for breakfast, along with large glasses of fresh orange juice squeezed by hand. The setting reminded Amber of the Garden of Eden, as butterflies flitted among tropical flowers and gentle trade winds wafted slow-moving clouds across the vast blue sky. The peace and tranquility of the place drenched her soul. "I drank it in like a thirsty sponge," she says.

Even so, Amber's paradise was marred by the harsh realities of her life. It's hard to imagine how it feels to suddenly go from a normal state of health and independence to finding yourself completely dependent on others, utterly incapable of doing for yourself even the most basic personal chores—like blowing your nose or going to the bathroom.

Amber did her utmost to buck up under the circumstances, but she hated being such a burden to others. It was, perhaps, the single most devastating aspect of the new circumstances of her life.

Amber struggled bravely to survive. But because of the abject turmoil of her broken heart, which she didn't feel she could share with anyone else, she began to withdraw into herself. That, of course, only made things worse. And without the degree of understanding necessary to perceive the depths of Amber's loneliness, loss, and anxiety, people around her began to misinterpret her withdrawal as simple self-pity.

But Amber doesn't indulge in self-pity for long; she's way too strong for that. What she was experiencing can best be described as a state of near-total emotional paralysis brought on by an enormous load of overwhelming stresses multiplied by the loss of her health, mobility, independence, career, marriage, and self-image in a very short period of time. It doesn't take a lot of insight to realize that it's a wonder she survived at all.

Back home in California, I was finding it increasingly difficult to cope with all the changes in my own life. I hadn't realized how much I depended on Amber to help me maintain my own equilibrium. Now that she was gone and now that the guilt and self-hatred were draining every ounce of self-respect from my soul, I fell deeper than ever into drugs and alcohol—and right smack into the arms of an understanding woman named Michelle.

I better back up for a minute, to the night before Amber was discharged from the hospital in California. She'd been trying to get in touch with me for hours that night, but I wasn't at home. I was out with Amber's best friend, Michelle. (That isn't her real name, of course.) Michelle had begun helping me with some of the practical details of life when Amber was so forcibly taken from me, and, well, one thing led to another . . .

The next day, as I brought Amber home from the hospital, I couldn't bring myself to tell her what had happened, so I just acted nonchalant. But Amber wasn't entirely fooled; a woman's intuition can be amazingly accurate. For the time being, however, she dismissed her concerns as nothing but an overdose of situational anxiety.

Chapter Seventeen

Lucifer's Coup d'Etat

As Amber's days in the Fijian garden passed into weeks, she began to miss the members of her family back in California very much. Each day she spent hours dreaming about Chris and Kathy and especially her precious little granddaughter, Kandace. Somehow, thinking of them always brought her thoughts back to me.

"Oh, how I missed Michael!" she remembers. "Even though he'd been negligent in my care and we had quarreled so often, I loved him and worried about what was happening in his life. Was he killing himself with drinking and drugs? Was he faithful to me, or was he spending time with someone else? Did he miss me half as much as I was missing him? How come he never called?"

One of the things that troubled her was the strange way her friend Michelle—who had accompanied her on the long flight from Los Angeles to Fiji—had reacted when Amber asked her to write me a letter telling me how very much she loved me. "Michelle broke down and sobbed and told me she couldn't write that letter," Amber recalls.

For some reason, Amber didn't ask why. But as she reflected on the incident over the ensuing days and weeks, things started coming together in her mind, and she grew increasingly suspicious. Even so, she was reluctant to believe the worst about her best friend and her husband. She had already been through so much; she just couldn't bring herself to imagine that Michelle and I could have been so cruel as to add the insult of infidelity to everything else I had dumped in her lap.

How could I do that? I've asked myself the question a million times since then. Even though I knew adultery is never the answer, the weakened condition of my will and spirit made it easy to capitulate to temptation. Besides, I reasoned, if God had wanted Amber and me to stay together, He wouldn't have allowed the accident to occur. It was as slipshod a rationale as any I've ever heard, but I bought it nonetheless. To be honest, I can't explain what I did; it was one of the biggest sins of my entire life. Adultery is never justifiable; it is the source of countless cases of misery and suffering in the world.

A few days after Michelle's emotional outburst, Amber's mother said something—an unintended slip of the tongue—and from that, Amber was able to infer the reason for Michelle's tears and my flippant mask of pretentious innocence and silence. "When I called Michael to ask about it, he wouldn't say a word," she remembers. "I got my answer right then."

It doesn't take a lot of imagination to understand why Amber would tell me later that when she finally put two and two together and figured out what had happened the night before her discharge from the hospital, she felt as though she'd been kicked in the stomach by a mule. "This was a private pain I couldn't share with anyone," she observes, "not even the members of my own family."

As a result, the reservoir of her love turned instantly to hatred. She stopped praying, she stopped believing, and she began to contemplate revenge. After losing so dramatically in the witchcraft debacle, Lucifer and his impish lieutenants savored the remarkable victory they had achieved by the far more commonplace strategy of "divide and conquer."

And why not? With one illicit tryst they had accomplished nearly every objective of their diabolical agenda for our marriage and our lives.

Chapter Eighteen

No Woman Is an Island

Remember Jesus' friends Mary, Martha, and Lazarus? As I look back over the years, I see a number of parallels between their story and ours. Like Mary, who saddened and embarrassed Martha and Lazarus by her conduct before she came to know Jesus, I was the source of enormous pain and resentment to Amber.

While I was back home in California searching for something to silence the torrent of accusing voices inside my head, Amber was struggling to reconnect with her own identity. Day after day a steady barrage of overheard conversations threatened to drain the last traces of hope and optimism from her soul. She began to feel more like an object than a person as she heard friends and family say things like "What a waste," "She's so young!" and "She had everything, but look at her now." There were times when she wanted to scream "I'm not a blob; I'm a person!"

To console herself, Amber would take stock of the faculties still under her conscious control. "I can still think," she reminded herself. "I still have feelings. I can make decisions. I just can't walk."

Whenever she was so discouraged that she felt like giving up, the Holy Spirit would bring texts of Scripture to her mind the way He had done that cruel night as she lay on the cold desert floor with a broken neck. " 'Come unto me, all ye that labour and are heavy laden, and I will give you rest,' " He would whisper in her mind. " 'Take my yoke upon you, and learn of me; for I am meek and lowly in heart: and ye shall find rest unto your souls. For my yoke is easy, and my burden is light' " (Matthew 11:28-30, KJV).

Even so, depression and despair continually assaulted the spark of determination and confidence that the Holy Spirit planted in her soul. Here she was, quadriplegic for the rest of her life, with a broken marriage and little, if any, reason to live. Her darling granddaughter was half a world away, and the man she loved more than anyone else in the world had betrayed her and driven a dagger through the center of her heart and soul.

People who have never been through a series of devastating experiences can't possibly imagine how hopeless it makes a person feel. Amber found herself constantly struggling for some kind of resolution to her problems—some way to bring closure to her misery, and a lasting sense of peace. She prayed, she cried, and she lashed out at everyone around her, but nothing produced the peace she was seeking.

One day, after a particularly angry tantrum, Amber finally realized that her dilemma was much too large for her to surmount. She finally accepted the fact that there was no way she would ever be able to dispel her sorrow on her own. "It was," she would admit later on, "as if the Holy Spirit had been standing aside for the longest time, patiently waiting for me to relinquish control and hand my problems entirely over to Him."

Once she did that, He began to speak. Not surprisingly, He picked up the very poignant words of Jesus recorded in Matthew 5:23, 24 and brought them to her attention. " 'If you bring your gift to the altar,' " Christ seemed to say directly to her, " 'and there remember that your brother has something against you, leave your gift there before the altar, and go your way. First be reconciled to your brother, and then come and offer your gift' " (NKJV).

"After what Michael has done to me?" she argued with God. "I didn't do anything to him, yet he nearly killed me, and then he had an affair! He did me wrong! You expect me to just *forgive* him for all that?"

Amber could hardly believe what the Spirit was asking her to do. "I can't do it, Lord," she insisted. "I just can't bring myself to forgive him."

Had she been dealing with a human psychiatrist instead of the Great Physician, she might have received some kind of gentle, understanding reply—maybe something like "Of course you're angry. You have every right to feel hurt and to hold a grudge, at least for now. But give it some time, and perhaps one day you can take the first baby steps towards letting go."

But the Holy Spirit took no such tactful approach. Not with Amber. Instead, the sweet, soft Wind that blows through John 3 with such delicate grace roared like a hurricane when confronting the iron strength of Amber's choleric will.

"How badly do you want eternal life?" the Spirit inquired. "Enough to forgive Michael for what he's done to you? Do you value your anger toward Michelle and him more than everlasting life?"

Then He drove the point home with one of the most difficult sayings Christ ever pronounced. It's found in Matthew 6:15: " 'If ye forgive not men their trespasses, neither will your Father forgive your trespasses' " (KJV).

Those are strong words. With all her heart, Amber wanted forgiveness for her sins. But how could she ever find the strength to forgive the man who destroyed her life? It didn't help matters one bit when the Holy Spirit reminded her that the kind of forgiveness God was looking for had to come from the heart.

How could she do it? How could a woman whose entire life had been ruined by the man she loved ever find the strength or even the willingness to forgive him *from the heart?* Obviously, that was more goodness than she could manufacture!

What happened next was nothing short of a miraculous internal transformation. The very moment Amber acknowledged to God that she was completely unable to do what He was asking her to do, she was immediately assured that all the help she needed was ready to swing into action on her behalf. For the first time in the entire conversation, the Holy Spirit moved from the role of formidable Challenger to that of Comforter and Friend. He turned her attention to a potent promise from Ezekiel 36:26, 27: " 'I will give you a new heart and put a new spirit within you; I will take the heart of stone out of your flesh and give you a heart of flesh. I will put My Spirit within you and cause you to walk in My statutes, and you will keep my judgments and do them' " (NKJV).

For the first time in months, Amber felt the peace she had been so desperately seeking. Suddenly, she was beginning to have hope. The Spirit had spoken; He had made an incredible offer that she could not— she would not—refuse.

The only question remaining was one of performance. *Can God deliver on a promise like that?* she wondered to herself.

She was about to find out.

Chapter Nineteen

The Sound of Chains Breaking

Looking back from this perspective, I'm ashamed of what I did to Amber. I can never forget the misery I brought to the woman I love. I can't begin to tell you how many times I've wished I could have been paralyzed instead of her.

While Amber was beginning to recover in Fiji, things were going from bad to horrendous for me. Feelings of intense self-hatred tore at the soft tissues of my soul like a pack of hungry wolves bent on devouring every remaining shred of my dignity and sanity. As days and nights whirled past in a devastating blur of inner rage and turmoil, I continued to turn to booze and drugs for escape. I was losing my mind.

The circumstances that lead people into addiction to artificial substances are many and varied, but for me, the sensation of being powerful once again and regaining control over my out-of-control life were the potent incentives that kept me hitting the bottle and ingesting narcotics by every possible means.

Despite all the mistakes I have made, if I could live my life over, I would do only one thing differently: I would start years earlier than I actually did to build a solid relationship with the Lord Jesus Christ. That has become my highest priority. I shudder when I think of the suffering Amber and I could have avoided had I done that right from the start. Nothing in my entire life—not drugs, not sex, not even the thrill of standing on stage before thousands of people—can even come close to the stability and satisfaction Christ has brought to my soul.

I feel sorry for people who think religion is a boring tradition or dispiriting obligation that limits their options and dampens their joy. They don't have a clue what resting in Jesus means. My standing in Christ and my ongoing relationship with Him are the greatest blessings I've ever known!

I don't mean to imply that all religion is healthy and good. People can get so stuck in forms and rituals that they miss the point. The point is to know Christ and go deep in the journey of faith with Him.

The Creator of this magnificent universe is anything but boring. He's also anything but the passive pushover of uninformed imagination. The Christ I know is not only the source of life, He's also the Man who challenged death to the ultimate showdown and walked away alive. A living relationship with that kind of Person is the most fulfilling and meaningful adventure available on this planet!

What always amazes me about Christ is the fact that He absolutely loves to take on the most difficult cases, such as the kid who can't get along with anyone else, the boy from the broken home who doesn't trust anyone, the girl whom everyone picks on because she doesn't fit in, or the person of any age or gender whose struggle for acceptance leads to one form of self-destructive behavior or another.

Another thing that always surprises me is the fact that Christ never censures us nor ridicules our weakness. For years I deceived myself into believing that I could handle booze and drugs. Because I was born with a vigorous physical constitution, I took my strength for granted. While my friends got drunk after just a few rounds of drinks, I could drink and smoke dope all night and still go to work sober in the morning. But I was only fooling myself. When the bill finally came due, it was more than I could pay.

As I've gotten to know Christ over the past decade and a half, I've discovered something ironic about the way He treats people. From what I've learned by searching the Bible and through His involvement in my life, I've come to realize that Christ never condemns the so-called "bad people" of the world. In that, He stands almost entirely alone. Turn on the radio or TV at any hour of the day or night, and you're almost certain to hear some thunder-breathing preacher railing against the homosexuals and abortionists of our day, or bashing the liberals for trying to decriminalize marijuana and pander to pornographic voyeurism via the media.

Please don't misconstrue this to mean that I think Christians should go soft on sin. That's not my intention at all; the Bible does take a very strong stand against sin of every sort. But we commit the worst sin of all when we embrace the notion that any of us have the right to throw stones in condemnation of anyone else. Oh how I wish that America's Christian leaders and politicians would wake up to this liberating discovery!

Christians need to realize that people are seldom, if ever, converted by having their sins exposed and lambasted from the pulpit. That only hardens hearts and entrenches skeptics in unbelief. People come to Christ when they see those who claim to be His followers openly accepting into their fellowship folks who are broken and imperfect. And this happens only when Christians are willing to confess candidly that they, like the drunk in the gutter and the streetwalker on the corner, are fallen human beings who wouldn't stand a chance of getting into heaven were it not for the mercy of the Son of God.

Unfortunately, however, the responses of many of the "saints" today are identical to those of the religious leaders two thousand years ago. Once those people discovered that Christ wouldn't condemn people who found themselves trapped in various forms of addictive lifestyles and behaviors, they criticized Him constantly. "This man is a friend of sinners!" they exclaimed. "He associates with prostitutes and publicans and thieves."

They were right—He did! And, thank God, He still does.

Folks who think they're entitled to God's blessings because of their good behavior are the hardest people in the world for God to save. Why? Because they're utterly blind to their desperate need of a Savior. That's why Jesus told them, "The tax collectors and prostitutes are going into the Kingdom of God ahead of you" (Matthew 21:31, TEV).

Do Jesus' words mean that Christians should treat social outcasts and moral rejects as if they were Christ Himself? Ask Mary Magdalene or the diseased man at the pool of Bethesda or the woman at the well. "Christ Jesus came into the world to save sinners." To treat even the worst of sinners with anything but the same love and courtesy that Jesus showed is high-handed treason against the gospel of grace!

So, the next item on the Holy Spirit's agenda was to open Amber's eyes to my true condition. He helped her stop perceiving me as a strong, in-control monster who had willfully injured her. "He pointed my attention to the dark spirit behind Michael and revealed that he was a captive to Satan's will," Amber would say later on. "Amazingly, the Holy Spirit even brought me to realize that what happened between Michael and Michelle had nothing to do with me!"

Once again, I'm amazed at the wisdom of Jesus. How could Amber—or anyone in her condition—ever come to the point of releasing such an enormous load of bitterness and resentment? Certainly not and most likely not even then without years of psychotherapy. Only the Lord could accomplish such a remarkable transformation! But He was just getting started.

"The next thing the Spirit taught me," Amber remembers, "is that even though Michael had done wrong, Jesus loved him anyway. Never once did He do or say anything to diminish the fact that Michael had brought great harm to me, but neither did He allow me to wallow in my sorrows once the time for healing had arrived."

All of a sudden, Amber felt the sweet breeze of peace blowing across the tortured landscape of her soul.

"The Holy Spirit said that even though the coin is lost, it doesn't lose its value in the sight of God. When I heard that, things began to change! Now I could look at Michael as a brother in Christ who had been misled by Satan. I could see that he was a slave to sin, all burdened down with shame and remorse. I knew he wasn't happy. I also knew I could forgive him. I can't begin to tell you what an enormous load was lifted from my heart when the Spirit brought me to that conclusion!"

I can't think of anything appropriate to say in response to that, except "Hallelujah!" and "Praise the Lord!" But I would like to share the lyrics to a song that one of Christ's ambassadors, Stacey D. Smallegan, wrote especially for Amber and me. It beautifully and unpretentiously captures the essence of what God has done in our lives. Amber and I cherish every verse. The song is entitled "A Prayer Across the Ocean."

A prayer across the ocean
brought me back to you,
heard by our precious Savior
whose love is tried and true.

Thank You, God, for not giving up on me.
Thank You, God, for my precious wife,

the woman who quietly prayed for me
and helped to save my life.

She will walk again when the Lord returns,
and her faith has helped me see
that Your grace can span the waters of the world
to save a lost sinner like me.
My gratitude goes up to You
in this song of praise.
You've unshackled me from all the things
that kept me in a daze.

I'm thankful, Lord, that through Your love,
our lives have been made new.
I do not know where we would be today
if it were not for You.

Your love is so astounding
that it would cross the sea,
sent up to You by children of faith
who knew You could set me free.

A prayer across the ocean—
what love, what faith, what power!
The same strong arms of love
that will hold us in our final hour.

Only You, Lord, would know
the beginning from the end.
You are the God of heavenly grace;
You are our faithful Friend.

We're thankful to Stacey for reminding us that God answers prayers
no matter how unlikely it seems that the person for whom they're offered
will ever respond.

I know something about hopeless persons. I'm living proof that Jesus
saves!

Chapter Twenty

At the Divine Embassy

The Sunday before Christ voluntarily died on the cross for our sins, He quoted a psalm of King David that reminds me of Amber's little nieces and nephews in Fiji. Of course, they're not little anymore—children have a way of growing up—but their story clearly demonstrates that a giant faith often comes in pint-sized bottles.

"Why don't you tell your disciples to be quiet?" the scribes and Pharisees had urged. "They're creating such a scene that the Romans are likely to arrest us all for disorderly conduct!"

Christ responded, "Have you never read the passage which says, 'Out of the mouth of babes and sucklings thou hast perfected praise'?" (See Matthew 21:16.)

To me, the idea that God leaves the really important work to babies and children makes a lot of sense. Adults complicate things too much.

Once the Holy Spirit brought Amber to the conclusion that she could forgive me from the heart, He called in the troops. Not surprisingly, His advance battalion was a group of children ranging in age from four to thirteen—her nieces and nephews.

"Auntie Amber," their spokesman would say as they traipsed in barefooted and smiling, "let's pray for Uncle Michael in America. And we can pray for cousin Chris and Kathy and Kandace and little Chris too."

Amber hadn't met little Chris yet. Chris and Kathy's baby son had come into the world after our accident and was happily exploring his new home in America while his Grandma Amber was living in Fiji. And oh, she wanted to meet him! Day after day, the thought that she had a brand-new grandbaby boy brought unspeakable joy and excitement to Amber's heart; especially now that the Holy Spirit had turned her hatred into love.

Tears would fill her eyes as the little prayer warriors lifted every member of her family to the throne of grace with the natural exuberance of childhood. Their innocence and sincerity must surely have brought joy to God's heart too, because shortly after they started to pray for me, He opened the way for heaven to work on our behalf. Things began to change for the better for Amber and me in a matter of a few short days.

For one thing, Amber moved into her Auntie Charlotte's home. This house was a large, three-bedroom structure with a veranda that overlooked the ocean. Tourists pay thousands of dollars for the privilege of basking in the spectacular beauty of the Fiji Islands, and there it was, right off Amber's front porch.

Auntie Charlotte, Amber's mother's sister, was an exceptional Christian woman who lived her faith in a variety of practical ways. Every morning the wonderful aroma of fresh bread baking in the oven flooded the house with its tantalizing perfume. And once everything was ready, Auntie Charlotte would wheel Amber out on the veranda to a delightful breakfast served in the grand tradition of the fine British hospitality seen in the South Seas. The sparkling white tablecloth, bouquet of colorful garden flowers, and heaping platters of delicious homemade bread and sweet tropical fruits was more than enough to activate the appetite and stimulate the salivary glands. Of course, the presence of butterflies and trees, trade winds and gentle waves didn't exactly detract from the atmosphere of joy and serenity either. The simplicity and beauty of that wonderful environment exerted a powerful healing influence on Amber's body, mind, and spirit.

Like Grandma Jackson, her Auntie Charlotte is a member of the Seventh-day Adventist Church. Would to God that every Christian would reflect as much of the love and kindness of Jesus as Auntie Charlotte did! She expressed His love in so many thoughtful ways. She would drop a fragrant gardenia on the dresser as she walked past Amber's window each morning. A little while later she would come into the room and read something positive and uplifting. And since there was no night light in Amber's room, Charlotte would light a kerosene lamp in the hall outside her door. She was constantly looking for ways to make life pleasant for others. What a remarkable, godly woman!

Charlotte's whole house seemed charged with an atmosphere of grace. Three small frames on the walls of Amber's room held texts of Scripture. Gradually, she committed them to memory. They couldn't have been more appropriate to the present circumstances of her life.

"I have learned, in whatsoever state I am, therewith to be content," the text of Philippians 4:11 (KJV) proclaimed.

Like Christ's command to forgive from the heart, this one seemed at first like a bit of a stretch to Amber, considering the recent events of her life. Nevertheless, she resolved to integrate its meaning into her heart with the help of her divine Healer.

Another of the apostle Paul's landmark declarations resonated in her spirit: " 'My grace is sufficient for you, for My strength is made perfect in weakness' " (2 Corinthians 12:9, NKJV).

OK, Lord, she thought. *I've got the weakness; You bring the strength. Let's see what You can do!*

But the familiar words of the third verse on the wall, Romans 8:28, seemed to defy logic. Even so, Amber was beginning to trust in God's promises, and she made up her mind to find out how this one applied to her as well: "We know that all things work together for good to those who love God, to those who are the called according to His purpose" (NKJV).

Amber soon discovered that in addition to Aunt Charlotte and the children, God had appointed another delegation of diplomats and ambassadors to assist in her journey to wholeness in Christ. And not all of them were human.

"Some nights when the moon was full or nearly full, the lovely moonlight would come streaming through my window," she remembers. "The round, gentle face of the moon looked like the smiling face of God to me. And the aroma of night-blooming flowers wafting in on the breeze was delectable beyond words. Oh, how sweet it was! The most expensive perfume on the planet is no match for such delicate fragrance."

As Amber lay awake at night, the old grandfather clock in the living room chiming out the hours and half-hours kept her company while everyone else slept. On those nights when she stayed awake into the wee hours of the morning, tropical birds would announce the soon-coming dawn with their happy chatter from the branches of nearby trees.

Shortly after daybreak, cousin Jack would bring his Bible and guitar into Amber's room, and they would make a joyful noise to the Lord. Later on, her sister Mona would stop by to massage Amber's muscles. "Her healing touch contributed as much as anything else to my recovery," Amber asserts.

Sharon, Wilma, and Rachel (the rest of Amber's sisters) and her brother David rounded out the diplomatic corps God assigned to Project Amber. No wonder she never had a chance to feel lonely or bored!

"Sharon was always bringing her children over to dance for me," Amber recalls. "When Wilma came to visit, we sat on the veranda and talked for hours. She was cheerful and witty, and we laughed a lot.

"I remember one day it was raining hard and I asked my helper to take me outside for a bath in the rain. Just then Rachel came running through the woods. 'I knew it!' she said. 'I just knew you'd be out in the rain!' "

Another time, David took Amber to the beach and set her down in the sand. She couldn't feel a thing with her feet, but she could discern its coarse, grainy texture with her hands. As Amber sat there reveling in the pure, sensate joy of sand running through her fingers, David climbed a tree. Moments later, he returned with an armful of green coconuts. As the two of them sipped the sweet nectar like happy children, they wondered how the tastes of heaven could surpass coconut milk on a day in the sun.

Amber gets a faraway look in her eye whenever she talks about those days in the islands. "It was a wonderful revelation to me," she says. "The accident brought our close-knit family even closer together."

Perhaps there's something to that promise in Romans after all.

Chapter Twenty-One

Helping Epeli

Every day, someone in the world comes face to face with devastating personal tragedy. A child is shot to death while waiting at a crosswalk for the light to change. A woman gets a call that her husband just suffered a massive heart attack and died. A man with a gambling addiction loses his home to card sharks in Vegas. A tornado rips across three Midwestern states, destroying thousands of homes and killing dozens of people.

From a purely numerical perspective, the situation is far worse in other parts of the world than it is in North America. Every night of the year hundreds of homeless children sleep on the streets of Brazil because their parents either don't want them, can't afford to feed them, or both. In Africa, thousands of orphans—many barely old enough to walk—roam the countryside scrounging for food to survive. Their parents died of AIDS because American and European drug manufacturers, who could have provided life-sustaining medications to arrest the ravaging disease and prolong lives for years, won't lift a finger to help. "It isn't financially viable," they explain. But in reality, they merely value profits over people.

Amber's friend Epeli knows something about institutional apathy. It nearly took his life in a Fiji hospital.

In the beautiful Fijian language, Epeli means "Abel," as in Cain and Abel. And like his famous namesake, Epeli got himself in serious trouble while innocently trying to do the right thing.

One afternoon, Epeli was watching the children in his village as they tried to field enough players for a game of rugby. As the father of six of those children, Epeli knew the value of outdoor recreation and was glad his kids were going to play. He really didn't intend to join the game himself, but the young people were one person short. "Come on," they insisted. "We need one more to make it a match."

At first, everything went smoothly enough. The breeze was blowing, palm trees were swaying, and everyone was having a good time. But all of a sudden, when Epeli's team joined hands to form a human barrier to prevent the other team from scoring, a sudden lunge caught Epeli off guard, and down he went. In the very next heartbeat, he was immobilized on the ground with a broken neck.

One day Aunt Charlotte asked Amber, "Why don't you come with me to the hospital and visit Epeli? I think you could cheer him up. He's a quadriplegic like you. He's been in the hospital five months, and I understand the poor man has bedsores from lying in one place for so long."

How could I possibly cheer someone up when I'm such a mess myself? Amber wondered to herself. But Aunt Charlotte was adamant that Amber could do Epeli some good, so Amber agreed to go along.

When they got to the hospital, Amber and Charlotte were appalled at what they saw. Even though Epeli was only in his thirties, he looked like a very old man.

"We couldn't believe it!" Amber exclaims. There he was, lying on his back with a single white sheet over his body. He was soaked with perspiration, and when Auntie Charlotte pulled the sheet back, they found a large bedsore running down the length of his spine. It was dripping a smelly discharge, and his tailbone was protruding through his skin. "I've never seen anything so horrible in my life!" Amber says.

Epeli's entire body was covered with sores. The flesh that used to cover his ankles and heels had been eaten away by neglect of the worst kind imaginable. He hadn't had a bath or even been turned one time in the entire five months he'd been a patient in the hospital. Not once!

When the nurse came back, Amber asked why Epeli was in such an unbelievably horrible condition. "Why haven't you moved him?" she demanded. "Why hasn't anyone been giving this man some exercise?"

Like the drug companies I mentioned at the beginning of this chapter, Epeli's nurse acted like she didn't care. The official explanation was that they were short-staffed and not trained in caring for quadriplegics.

Amber burned with righteous indignation. When the doctor came in to see Epeli a few minutes later, Amber told her what the nurse had said. Then she asked her why no one had bothered to exercise Epeli. To

Amber's astonishment, the doctor said she didn't know anything about exercising long-term disabled patients. Unlike the nurse, however, she did seem genuinely concerned and allowed Amber to teach her several of the exercises she had learned during her physical therapy sessions at Saint John's Hospital in California.

When they got home that evening, Aunt Charlotte asked Amber what she thought of the idea of bringing Epeli home to stay with them. "We have an extra bedroom," Charlotte said, "and it hurts me to see him dying by the inch. I think we could help him."

This is crazy, Amber thought to herself. *Auntie is an old woman. How could she possibly care for two quadriplegics?* Nevertheless, she could sense the strength of Charlotte's faith and resolve. Resistance seemed futile. "Sure," she found herself replying. "Why not?"

Don't ask me how, but Aunt Charlotte got the doctor's permission to let Epeli and his wife move into the spare bedroom in her home. The next item of business was to instruct his wife how to bathe and catheterize Epeli and massage his aching muscles and joints. Before long, all the exercises and therapy routines Amber had learned in the hospital were called into play.

Epeli fainted the first time they gave him a shower. He hadn't had one for so long that it was a shock to the systems of his body. But Aunt Charlotte had given her word that the injured man would receive the best possible care, and she went to work with a determination that made the processes of death and decay run the other way.

For one thing, she made sure Epeli got plenty to eat. In an age when so many people grow up on junk food, the importance of wholesome natural foods prepared in a way that retains maximum vitamin and mineral content is greatly overlooked. Not by Auntie Charlotte, however. In her kitchen, things were done right. She also made sure Epeli drank plenty of fresh, clear water to assist the cells of his body in the important tasks of discharging wastes and restoring vitality.

The next weapons in her arsenal were two other natural healers that, unfortunately, are too often neglected in the war against disease: fresh air and sunlight. Auntie Charlotte saw to it that Epeli spent some time every day outdoors in the sun.

As a result of the love and dedication of Auntie Charlotte and other members of her family, Epeli began to improve dramatically. The first thing to change was his attitude. Instead of just waiting to die, Epeli began to have hope. He could feel the difference between the neglect he had received at the hospital and the positive, proactive care he was getting at Auntie Charlotte's. For the first time in months he began to smile. And two weeks later, the bedsores showed visible signs of starting to heal. Like Amber, he was on the road to recovery.

When the doctor stopped by to check on Epeli a few days later, she was shocked at how rapidly he had improved. When everyone went out on the veranda to talk, Epeli's sister broke down in tears.

"What kind of angel are you?" she asked Auntie Charlotte. "You take a dying man into your home and you're not even related to him! He doesn't even belong to your church, yet you nurse him back from the brink of the grave."

I'll never forget Auntie Charlotte's response. Even though I wasn't there to hear it in person, I can just imagine the scene as she leaned forward and clasped her hands over her heart to express the beautiful emotion of her soul. "No," she said, "I'm the one who's been blessed by all this. To see Epeli respond to treatment and prayer—to see him go from skin and bones to a man with healthy flesh and bright eyes—that is more of a reward than I can ever say. It has brought pure joy to my heart. It's the way Jesus treated people." Then she went on to say that true happiness comes from serving your fellow human beings and that by focusing on Epeli, she had also received healing.

Epeli had been at Auntie Charlotte's for only a month when the doctor authorized his release back to his own home. She had never seen anyone recover so fast.

As for Amber, she'll always be grateful to Auntie for teaching her such a practical lesson in true happiness. "Her daily life and concern for others taught me what Christianity is really all about," she told me later. "God is so good! He provided new experiences and sent new people into my life and led me step by step down the Christian path. Oh, how I praise His name!"

However, Amber knew she couldn't spend the rest of her life in that environment of peace and beauty, even though she was surrounded by the friendliest people on the face of the earth. It wasn't that they wouldn't have been happy to care for her the rest of her life. The problem was that she was missing me and the other members of her family back in California. After all I'd done to her, she still loved me and wanted to see me again.

That's when the Spirit prompted me to pick up the phone and call.

Chapter Twenty-Two

Silent Voice, Loud Impact

The term "drug abuse" is an odd combination of words—sort of like "healthy suicide." In truth, there is no safe way (except under a doctor's orders) to use narcotic drugs without abusing them. They are designed for carefully controlled medical applications, and any usage at all outside those boundaries is an invitation to personal destruction.

After Amber got on the plane and left me, I fell deeper and deeper into a desperate cycle of addiction and fear. Everywhere I went, I thought people were talking about me behind my back. They weren't, of course, but that didn't stop me from thinking they were. I was entering a dangerous realm on the fringes of insanity.

As my paranoia worsened, I started seeing things that weren't really there. From the corner of my eye, I watched stationary objects move from place to place. They'd stand still when I looked at them, only to move again the moment I looked away.

Halfway around the world, things really were beginning to move, but in an entirely different way. Not only had God brought Amber to the point of surrendering her anger and opening her heart to the healing power of love and forgiveness, but He also kept moving on the hearts of my little nieces and nephews in Fiji to pray for me—to pray specifically that the Holy Spirit would work inside my heart and mind to break the addictions that held me powerless in their grasp.

Almost imperceptibly, things began to change in my thinking. Several nights in a row, as I was getting high with my so-called friends, the Lord spoke to me. While I was smoking marijuana and snorting cocaine, I would suddenly hear a quiet voice saying, *"Michael, I love you. What are you doing here?"*

I've heard voices before. If you take drugs long enough, you begin to experience extrasensory perception. In fact, the controlled use of hallucinogenic drugs has been a part of shamanistic ritual and primitive spiritualism for thousands of years precisely because of its power to induce bizarre mystical experiences and a heightened awareness of invisible spiritual forces.

But on this particular evening, the Voice I heard was nothing like those other voices. Instead of sounding deranged or intimidating, it was calm and logical. It told me, in no uncertain terms, that I was living in a world of danger and there was nothing I could do to escape. It told me, though, that Someone was willing to set me free if only I would allow Him.

That definitely got my attention! Someone was jamming my frequency to deliver a message of extreme importance. He made it clear that I was fast approaching the point of no return, and, apparently, He wasn't willing to let that happen without offering help.

"This is my last night of using drugs," I suddenly announced to my friends. "Tomorrow I'm going to give my life completely to Jesus Christ."

"There he goes again," they said.

Chapter Twenty-Three

A Cry in the Dark on a Sunny Day

Early in the morning two days after my declaration, my guilty conscience ripped into me like a Doberman pinscher on steroids. "Thought you were gonna become a Christian?" it sneered. "Sort of blew that idea last night, didn't you? What makes you think God can help a loser like you? You're a disaster, Michael! You almost killed your wife, your life is in chaos, and now you're listening to a voice that says there's an easy way out.

"How delusional can one guy get? There's no such thing as an easy way out! People go through years of therapy and detox. Some of them manage to break free for a while only to relapse back into a living hell when the going gets tough. Others drift into a permanent state of depression for the rest of their lives. Thousands more decide to take the offramp and check out for good. There are no guarantees for guys like you. The only way you'll ever get out of here is in a body bag!"

I knew *that* voice well. Night and day for months on end it had been torturing me with relentless reminders of the suffering I had caused my wife. I was getting desperate! I couldn't stand the pain another day.

To make things worse, Chris hated my guts for what I had done to his mother. He and Kathy were living with me, and even though he was my stepson, I needed his support and approval. But because of what my drug habit had done to his mother—not to mention the lifestyle I was living now—there was no way he would show me the respect that I craved. That hurt me a lot.

I stumbled out to the living room one morning after yet another hellacious night of drugs and despair. My brain was fried, and I guess I must have looked horrible. I sat on the couch trying to clear my head. I hoped the warm California sunlight streaming in through the window would help.

About that time my little granddaughter Kandace came bouncing down the hall. She and her brother, Christopher, have always been the apples of my eye. The moment Kandace saw me, a big smile danced across her face, and she ran down the hall with her arms open wide. "Grandpa!" she laughed. "Grandpa!"

But when she got close enough to see the leering, insane expression on my face and the dilated pupils of my eyes, she stopped dead in her tracks. Then her smile turned to a raw expression of horror and disgust, and she let out a shriek of terror and ran the other way to find her mother.

What's wrong? I wondered to myself. *Do I really look that bad?*

I don't know whether or not you've ever heard the phrase "busted and disgusted," but that's exactly how I felt. I stumbled into the bathroom and stared at the face in the mirror. Could that hideous image really be me? I hated what I saw. I hated the man I had allowed myself to become. More than anything, I hated the fact that I had let myself degenerate to the point where little Kandace couldn't bear to be around me.

For the first time in decades, I saw what drugs had done to me. I was no longer strong; I was nothing but a strung-out junkie, hopelessly addicted and completely powerless to save myself. I was a desperate, ruined man who was standing just inches away from insanity or death.

"Dear God!" I cried out loud as I dropped to my knees on the bathroom floor. "What have I done? My own granddaughter is afraid of me. I'm an awful mess. I've tried to stop using drugs so many times, Lord, but I just can't seem to find the way. I need Your help. Will You please help me?"

The moment I finally realized my complete hopelessness and surrendered to the Lord with my whole heart and soul, He took over and turned my life around. Sometimes religion seems so complicated, but at its essence it's extremely simple: God can't help us until we come to realize that there is nothing we can do to save ourselves.

If you'll search the Scriptures, you'll see that's how it always works. Whenever a person reaches the point of willingly turning to the Lord

Jesus Christ, God gives the gift of salvation, and the person begins a whole new way of life. No wonder Jesus called it being "born again"! The person has just been carried over from spiritual death to everlasting life.

Had it not been for the Spirit's quiet assurance that God still loved me and was perfectly able to save me from my addictions and release me from my staggering load of confusion and guilt, I would have given up and died a long time ago. A person can only endure so much. As it was, I rose from my knees a whole new man. The sun was shining, my face was beaming, and for the first time in decades I was free.

Some people find a way out of the living hell of addiction and despair through twelve-step programs such as Alcoholics Anonymous and Narcotics Anonymous or through one of the other peer-support groups. Those organizations have done a world of good for thousands of people, and I have the highest respect for the work they do. But I found freedom through the one-step program.

What is the one step I took? The Holy Spirit brought me to the point of crying out in desperation to the Lord Jesus Christ, and He took it from there.

Did it work? Let's put it like this: I took that one step in 1988, and I haven't used drugs once since that day. Not even once.

As impossible as it seems to people who haven't experienced Jesus' life-changing love for themselves, He saved my life and set me free that morning when my granddaughter's terrified outburst disabled my defenses and brought me to my knees.

Jesus made a proclamation all the people of the world need to claim as their own. "If the Son makes you free," He said, "you shall be free indeed" (John 8:36, NKJV).

He did, and I am. Thank You, Jesus!

Chapter Twenty-Four

Messy Diapers

For the past ten years, during my concerts throughout the United States and Canada, Australia, the West Indies, and Europe, I've been telling the story of my miraculous deliverance from drugs and alcohol to thousands of people. Every time I tell it, someone comes away with new hope in their heart. It's been my pleasure to witness profound changes in the lives of people who have sought the Lord for themselves.

Sometimes the miracles God works in the lives of these people are every bit as dramatic and impossible as the ones He's constantly working for me. But not always. Sometimes people who turn to the Lord find that they still struggle with addictions. Sometimes they don't get the miraculous turnaround they came seeking. Sometimes they continue to fight old habits for years.

What makes the difference? There are many factors involved in the struggle for freedom from addiction, and the story is different for every person. But God is still willing—always willing—and able to forgive and to heal. So, people who suffer from a sense of failure because they don't immediately gain complete victory after they surrender to the Lord need not lose hope. Christ died to *save* sinners, not to condemn them. He never attacks anyone because of their weakness or addiction. Other people may condemn them, and they may condem themselves, but Jesus never does. Even in our darkest hours, we are completely forgiven, totally accepted, and unconditionally loved by the Lord.

Folks who are discouraged at their failures—people who just lost another battle with drugs, alcohol, lust, pornography, anger, abusiveness, or any other harmful habit—may come to the Cross just as they are and discover that the justice of God has been completely satisfied by the righteous life and atoning sacrifice of His Son. So let the lonely and depressed come to Him! Let the hopeless and despondent come to Christ! Let those who struggle with dark supernatural forces come boldly to the throne of grace, for "they shall find mercy," as Paul reminds us, "and grace to help in time of need."

That's what Jesus meant when He said, "Whosoever believeth in him should not perish, but have everlasting life" (John 3:16, KJV). *Whosoever* is the most inclusive word in all the world. It means that God is willing to accept anyone and everyone on the basis of Christ's death on the cross. Since the day Jesus died, no one on the planet has the right to deny anyone else unlimited access to the love and transforming power of God.

If I may venture to speculate, I would guess that some people don't find deliverance when they seek it from God because they are still trying, in some way, to do something to help God save themselves. And no wonder! From the time we're little kids, we are constantly assaulted with the regrettable notion that God helps those who help themselves.

That notion is true in some areas of life. God won't write a paper for me. I've got to sit down and put my thoughts on paper. He won't go to school for me or earn my degree. I've got to go to class, dialogue with the instructor, study the textbook, and do my assignments. There are many things I've got to do for myself.

But in the spiritual arena, God takes the opposite approach. When it comes to breaking the cycle of addictions and other harmful behavior patterns, God helps those who *can't* help themselves. And that flies directly in the face of everything we know. We cling to the values of self-reliance and independence. We tie our own shoes and dress ourselves. We learn to catch the bus or develop the skills to drive. By the time we reach our teens, we're so self-sufficient that we qualify as first-class "do-it-ourselfers."

But that's not how we started out. I've known lots of independent people in my life, but I've never met any who changed their own diapers as a baby. Our earliest experiences of life involved letting someone else feed us, clothe us, and clean us. We couldn't even get rid of the gas in our stomachs until someone else picked us up and burped us. All we could do was eat, sleep, cry, and mess our pants. Our very survival depended completely on the actions of someone else.

In the spiritual life, we get into trouble whenever we try to hang on to the illusion of control. When Christ said we must become like little children in order to enter the kingdom of heaven, He didn't mean we have to talk, think, and act like babies. He meant that just as a baby is entirely at the mercy of someone else, so we are dependent on the loving God who knew all about our problems and addictions long before we were born, yet chose to love us, nurture us, and care for us even while we were still making a mess of our lives. "While we were yet sinners, Christ died for the ungodly" is the way Paul explained it.

In chapter 28 I'll discuss the one thing people can do to nurture their own souls on a regular basis, but for now, let me appeal to all of us, myself included, to stop judging others—and to stop condemning ourselves when we try and fail. Instead, let's practice the art of accepting each other and respecting ourselves, because God accepted us the day Christ paid the price for our sins on the cross.

In Romans 8:1, the apostle Paul, whose deliverance episode was every bit as remarkable as my own, wrote something incredibly liberating. He wrote, "There is therefore now no condemnation to those who are in Christ Jesus" (NKJV).

Someone had a hard time believing such a wonderful statement could possibly be true, so he took it upon himself to add the following words to the verse: "who do not walk according to the flesh, but according to the Spirit." That isn't what Paul meant. What he wrote was the brief, but powerful first part of the verse: "There is therefore now no condemnation to those who are in Christ Jesus." Period. End of sentence.[1]

If you believe in Christ, that remarkable promise includes you. You are set free from condemnation. So am I. We are now free to go and live a life of peace with God.

If you're struggling right now with a habit you can't break, get down on your knees and thank the Lord that you are under grace, not condemnation. Then ask Him to deliver you from addiction. Admit that you're powerless to resist its control over your life, and ask Him to give you victory. Then believe that He will. And if you should fall into sin again, remind yourself that Jesus is your Advocate with the Father. He's your Defense Attorney as well as your Savior and Friend, and you're not under condemnation, no matter what Lucifer says!

It doesn't matter who you are, what you've done, or how frequently you've failed in your struggle to go free: God loves you just the way you are, and He's working overtime to help you comprehend, receive, and walk in the light of the everlasting victory His Son obtained for you on the cross.

You may be temporarily defeated. You may be discouraged, guilty, powerless, and ashamed. Take courage, my friend! Your case isn't hopeless, and you are *not* condemned.

Jesus saves!

---

¹See just about any modern translation.—Editor.

Chapter Twenty-Five

Please Don't Hang Up!

Forgiveness is never an issue with God. It's His very nature; it defines the essence of His personality. But people sometimes have a hard time forgiving each other.

It doesn't take a spiritual giant to let someone off the hook for taking our parking spot or bumping into us by accident in the grocery store. But forgiving someone who has hurt us significantly or messed up our life is an altogether different matter.

After Christ lifted the huge load of guilt and condemnation from my shoulders that morning on the bathroom floor, I felt an immediate change come over me. I opened my eyes and knew at once that nothing would ever be the same. I knew God had accepted me and forgiven me. More than that, I knew that He had instantaneously set me free from decades of addiction and chemical dependency.

But I also knew Amber was going to have a hard time believing that I wasn't just playing a new variation on the same old game. Nevertheless, as my mind became clearer with each passing day, I began to long for the love and companionship of my wife.

Did I have the right to ask her to trust me again? Not a chance! Because of my foolishness, in one horrifying moment she had gone from being a vivacious young woman with a bright future to someone facing a life of confinement in a wheelchair. And to make matters worse, I had hardly even told her that I was sorry. Instead, I'd slipped further into drugs, neglected her needs, become cruel and abusive, and left her completely unprotected. And after all that, I'd had a one-night stand with her best friend! What could I possibly say or do to convince her that I had changed? The obvious answer was nothing.

The more I thought about it, the more I realized that I had absolutely no right to expect Amber to forgive me. She had a million reasons to hate me. I didn't deserve her forgiveness. Nevertheless, deep in my heart I knew I could never be complete without her. She was the love of my life! I began to pray that God would speak to her heart about me in a way that would soften her attitude. "Please help me, Lord," I begged. "Help Amber be willing to take me back and give me another chance!"

Day after day, night after night, I dreamed of calling her on the phone and saying, "Please come home." I rehearsed everything I'd say and tried to imagine every possible response she might throw at me. Somehow, though, I always chickened out just before I actually dialed her number. I knew that now, with Jesus in my heart, we could make a new start. I was certain that we could reestablish our home on the solid foundation of Christ and His Word. But what if she said No? Even though I was growing stronger in the Lord every day, I knew I wasn't ready for Amber to reject me.

Until the day I die, I will never forget the wave of panic that swept over me when I finally got up my nerve and dialed her number. As I sat there listening to the ringing on the other end of the line, I wondered whether I'd have the strength to say Hello if she answered. It was only the power of God that kept me from hanging up.

And then, the next thing I knew, there she was. And just like that, it was time to risk everything for the woman I loved.

"Hi, Honey," I managed to blurt out. "This is Michael. Please don't hang up. Can we talk?"

After a painfully long silence, she finally said, "Sure. What's on your mind?"

The way I saw it, this wasn't the time to beat around the bush. I came straight to the point. "Amber," I said, "I'm so lonesome without you. I need you. I love you. Won't you please come home?"

There was another long pause. Amber hadn't been expecting anything like this—not so soon, anyway. She caught her breath and rolled the idea around in her mind. "I don't know, Michael," she finally managed to say. "I've given my life fully to Jesus. I'll have to think about it."

Then she continued, "If I were to say Yes, I would want our home to be founded on Jesus Christ. He'd have to be the Head of our home."

I could hardly believe my ears! What Amber was saying told me that she'd found freedom from hatred and bitterness in the very same place where I'd discovered the source of freedom from addiction and condemnation—in the merciful, loving arms of the Lord Jesus Christ. Now it was my turn to tell her what Christ had done for me. This time it was her turn to be shocked.

I don't remember what else we talked about; Amber probably asked how Kandace and Christopher were doing, and I probably said they were fine. But I do remember how the conversation came to an end. We'd been talking for over an hour when Amber finally told me that despite all the pain I had caused her, she'd found the strength in Christ not only to forgive me but also to give me another chance.

It's a good thing Chris and Kathy and the kids weren't home when I hung up that phone. I broke into such wild, spontaneous singing that they'd have thought for certain that I had lost my battle to stay clean and sober. I felt like I was floating ten feet off the floor—but, praise the Lord, drugs had absolutely nothing to do with it.

Amber was coming home!

Chapter Twenty-Six

Ain't Grandkids Grand!

The way Amber remembers it, she didn't know what to say when I asked her to come back home. She'd been in Fiji eight months to the day when she took my call. She had made significant progress in her relationship with God and had taken great strides along the road to physical and emotional recovery from the accident. She had even forgiven me. Nevertheless, my question caught her off guard. *Way* off guard.

"Even though I longed for Michael and wanted to feel his strong arms holding me, I still didn't have a ready answer," she remembers. "I knew about his drugs and drinking and even about his affair with Michelle, but until he called, I hadn't known a thing about his change of heart."

There was so much to consider. What if it was just an act? What if I was faking the whole conversion story just to get Amber to come back home and give me money to buy drugs? I did my best to assure her that I had completely surrendered my life to Christ and that I genuinely desired to start over. I promised her that Christ had taken my craving for drugs away and that I was living clean and sober.

"I don't know, Michael," she said. "I'm not sure it could work. I can't afford to compromise my relationship with Christ. It means everything to me!"

For the better part of an hour, I explained to Amber that I truly believed that with God's help, we could make it work. I told her about the crisis in my life—about the fact that it took the fear in the eyes of a child to show me the mess I had become. And I told her about my desperate prayer on the bathroom floor. I told her that God had spoken directly to me two nights before that fateful morning and that He had promised me a whole new way of life if only I would give the whole tangled mess to Him. I assured her that with God's help I aimed to do what was right for the rest of my life.

In one way, Amber should have seen it coming. She and half the people in the Fiji Islands had been praying for me night and day! OK, maybe not half, but a large number, nevertheless. But when the miracle actually occurred, she didn't know what to think.

From her point of view, Amber was nothing if not a realist. "I realized," she recalls, "that so far as the world was concerned, the odds were all stacked against us. I knew it wouldn't be easy; in fact, I understood that it was next to impossible. But I could tell that Jesus really was on our side. I finally told Michael the only way we could pull it off was with a love triangle."

Now it was my turn to be shocked. *A love triangle?* I wondered. That sounded like the worst arrangement for us. But when Amber explained that Jesus Christ was going to be the third party in our marriage, I agreed wholeheartedly. We both knew He was our only hope.

I can scarcely remember what happened next. When Chris, Kathy, Kandace, and baby Christopher got home, I told them about the phone call and broke the news that Amber was coming home. They were as shocked and surprised as I was—and, understandably, not totally convinced it was the right thing for her to do. But they were very excited about seeing her again.

When Amber was wheeled off the plane, we had an incredibly joyous reunion! We cried a little and laughed a lot. Baby Christopher was six months old. He had never seen his Nana, and she commenced that very moment to spoil him in a very grandmotherly way. Little Kandace, who was just turning two, talked all the way home. She would prove to be one of the most effective therapists God assigned to aid Amber's recovery upon her return to California.

Amber and I were sharing a house with Chris and his family. A few minutes after I left for work the morning after Amber's return, Kandace came knocking at our bedroom door. "Nana, Nana," she inquired, "may I come in?"

No sooner had Amber said Yes than Kandace climbed right up in bed with her. This sweet little child understood her role very clearly; she was her Nana's constant companion, and that's all there was to it!

A few minutes later, Kathy came in with Kandace's clothes and a diaper. "Better let me change your diaper and dress you!" she said.

"No, no!" Kandace replied. "Nana is going to dress me."

As the two adults exchanged bemused glances, Kathy told Kandace she wasn't sure Amber could do it. "Nana's hands don't work very well," she explained.

"Oh, yes she can! Yes she can!" Kandace insisted. "I'll help her!"

Kathy looked at Amber and shrugged. "OK," she agreed. "You two work it out."

Amber hardly knew what to think. There she was, lying flat on her back, and somebody else had just declared that she was going to change a diaper—somebody named Kandace, to be precise. Amber was irritated. In fact, if anyone other than Kandace had presumed to make such an unreasonable demand of her, Amber would have responded in anger. But Kandace was two years old and cuter than the day is long, and, well, what was a nana to do? You try telling your two-year-old rehab coordinator that you're not going to cooperate with the program of therapy that she's marked out!

Accomplishing the task wasn't easy. Because Amber had only minimal use of her arms and no use of her legs, she had to struggle heroically just to sit up in bed. When she finally made it, Kandace lay down beside her and guided Amber's hands to the fastener tabs on the diaper. With a great deal of effort, Amber fumbled to close the first tab, but it slipped out of her grasp. She tried again and again, and all the while, Kandace was taking her role very seriously. "You can do it, Nana!" she encouraged. "Keep trying. I know you can do it!"

Amber was getting fatigued. Nevertheless, she gritted her teeth and made progress an inch at a time. "I was going to fasten her diaper if it killed me!" she says, laughing now.

It took the two of them almost half an hour, but they finally got the job done. When Kandace had her diaper and her play clothes on, Amber flopped back on the pillow, exhausted but elated.

That morning's work proved to be just the beginning of an everyday ritual that cemented the bond between Kandace and her nana and helped Amber grow stronger than she ever imagined possible.

From that day on, Amber and Kandace's days together were filled with activity. After Amber got Kandace dressed, the two of them spent the rest of each day playing, reading, eating, talking, and taking naps.

Amber was Kandace's teacher, playmate, and counselor—or was it the other way around? All I know is that I've never seen such a close relationship between a nana and her granddaughter.

One day, Kandace decided Amber wasn't getting enough exercise. "Nana," she said, "you sit on the edge of the bed and touch your toes."

What is she saying? Amber wondered to herself. *What can a two-year-old possibly know about exercise?* Instead of refusing, however, she merely asked Kandace a question: "And what if Nana falls off the bed?"

"Don't worry," Kandace replied. "If you do, I'll catch you." And with that, she pulled her pink plastic chair to the side of Amber's bed and sat down. "Just put your hands on my knees," she said confidently.

Amber began to argue with the Lord. *Is this really from You?* she wondered. *Are You trying to teach me through this adorable child?*

Since there was no response from the Throne, Amber elected to give it a go. Once more, at Kandace's insistence, she began to struggle. "I finally got to the edge of the bed and sat up," she remembers. "After that, it was just a short distance farther to bend over and touch my toes. I felt triumphant beyond words!"

"Nana, you did it! You did it!" Kandace enthused, dancing around the room. "I knew you could do it!"

"Yes, Darling, I did it!" Amber affirmed. "Thanks to you and Jesus, I did it. Now you are my physical therapist."

Today, Amber and I continue to enjoy a wonderful relationship with all our grandchildren. Not only Kandace and Christopher, but now Kayla too fills our days with delight. She came along six years after Christopher was born. Even when she was barely a toddler, she wanted to help Amber, too. She put Amber's socks on for her and brushed her hair. Then she would sing beautiful songs. Amber was delighted.

Speaking of music, when I travel around the country singing praises to the Lord, Kayla often comes on stage with me and sings a solo or two and joins me for a duet. From the time she was a toddler, she loved to come into the studio and watch me sing. Right now, Miss Kayla Louis is working on her second CD. I imagine that one of these days she'll be letting me sing a number or two at her concerts! She's got all the makings of a contemporary Christian artist, and I'm proud to say she learned it all from me. (OK, so that's stretching it a bit, but I did teach her everything I know about singing!)

Before I close this chapter, I dare not leave out the cute little things Christopher did to help Amber recover. Now that he's all grown up, he won't be particularly excited about hearing them again, but that's why the Lord made grandparents—somebody's got to do the bragging around here!

Baby Christopher loved to sleep with Amber at night. Just before dozing off, he would roll over and blow kisses her way. Then he'd say, "I love you, Nana!" Could anything be sweeter? You tell me.

If you've got kids or grandkids around your place, don't forget to tell them you love them every day. In this era when kids feel such enormous pressure to get involved in drugs, sex, and the occult at an early age, love, understanding, and appropriate boundaries can make all the difference.

Chapter Twenty-Seven

Headed Toward Divorce—Again and Again

I'd like to tell you that everything turned out just fine when Amber got back from Fiji. I'd love to pretend there were no cross words, no arguments, no stubborn contests over who was in charge. But I'd be lying if I did.

Amber and I fully agreed, before we consented to share our story with the world, that if we were going to tell it at all, we'd have to tell the truth. Here goes.

We both had the best of intentions. However, despite the fact that we knew we were going to have to depend entirely on God to make our marriage work, we didn't always do it. Every issue has two sides, and we both did some pretty selfish things. Along the way, we learned that adults can throw temper tantrums just like children do.

"One day I got so mad at Michael," Amber confesses, "that I flung myself off the bed just to make a point. The impact nearly broke my toe.

"Another time, I decided to walk out on him in the middle of an argument. I was so mad that I forgot to check the brakes on my wheelchair. It flipped over, and I landed with a loud, hard thud on the floor. *Amber,* I thought to myself, *you just regained the use of your hands. Do you want to break them again?*

"Michael picked me up and set me on the bed, but I immediately threw myself on the floor again and crawled into the living room, where

I cried myself to sleep. To his credit, Michael brought a blanket and covered me up."

I appreciate the way Amber sometimes makes me look like a saint, but that's not the whole story. We're two strong-minded individuals with plenty of issues of our own. Amber deals constantly with pain and the frustration of not being able to do the things most people take for granted. And even though I know the Lord forgave me, even though I know Amber doesn't hold it against me, thinking of what I did to her still tears me up. Every so often the old self-condemnation sneaks in, and before I know it, I'm edgy, cranky, and insecure.

There were days when it seemed we were headed for the divorce court every half hour. Sometimes the devil would convince me that I was a very good boy to be so kind and patient with Amber. Then I'd start to feel superior, and, as Christ constantly told the Pharisees, that's always a recipe for relational and spiritual disaster.

Unless you've been living in a cave the past hundred years, you already know that marriage is difficult in today's environment. Somebody somewhere is always having an affair or slamming the door in someone else's face. It's a wonder so many folks do manage to stay married in this broken, mixed-up world of ours.

Instead of copping out, Amber and I decided to follow the Holy Spirit's leading. Every time we wanted to throw in the towel, we'd surrender ourselves to the Lord. He led us into the habit of daily Bible study and prayer and even kept us going to church. We didn't always want to, but He kept insisting, and who were we to say No?

After a while, we found it easier to turn to the Lord with each new problem. Whenever we did, He always led us to a successful resolution of our problems and a greater sense of peace and trust.

Did we get it right all the time?

No.

Do we now?

Of course not. We still have to ask God to forgive us and to restore harmony to our relationship. But He always comes through, and things are much better than they used to be.

Even in those first crucial weeks and months after Amber returned home, every time we thought divorce was the answer, the Holy Spirit kept suggesting He had something better in mind for us.

Chapter Twenty-Eight

A Bag of Wet Cement on Your Back

What would you do if you knew tonight was going to be your last night on earth? Eat your favorite food? Listen to your favorite music? Pray like never before?

On His last night alive, Jesus chose to teach. He'd been trying to teach His disciples a particular lesson for the better part of three years, but they still hadn't grasped the concept. So, on that fateful night, as they walked from the upper room to the Garden of Gethsemane, Christ explained once again how to succeed in the Christian life. The secret is called "sticking with the Vine."

As anyone who has ever tried to follow Christ for any length of time can tell you, the Christian life is a series of impossibilities. Not mere difficulties. Outright impossibilities.

Why? Because everything Christ taught us—whether it was loving our enemies or surrendering our thoughts, motives, and actions to the will of God—directly contradicts the inclinations of human nature. My impulse is never to forgive my enemy and turn the other cheek; I'd rather smack him upside the head. And I don't just naturally feel like surrendering control to the will of God either. I'd rather call my own shots.

But we can't just go with our gut if we want to live as Christians. Nobody will ever take Christ seriously if we who claim to be His followers always respond according to the whims of fallen human nature.

So, how does the impossible become a reality in the life of the believer?

To understand how that happens, we first must come to realize— usually through a long and frustrating process of trial and error— that we humans have no power to change the motives of our hearts and souls. In Jeremiah 13:23 we are reminded that it's no more possible for us to change from wanting to do evil to wanting to do good than it is for us to change the color of our skin. No amount of willpower, positive thinking, education, or effort can turn us from selfish to holy.

An old adage says, "Never try to teach a pig to sing. It wastes your time and irritates the pig." That adage fits the attempt to reform our motives—only we soon discover it's not a pig we're dealing with; our sinful nature is really a beast, a dragon, a monster.

If we are to grow in grace, God must work upon our souls. That's the meaning of John 6:28, 29. The people of Jesus' day asked Him the most important question in the world: "What must we do to do the works God requires?"

Jesus' reply says it all: "The work of God is this: to believe in the one he has sent" (NIV).

That's all there is to it! Believing in Jesus is the way to grow in grace. It's also the way to conquer long-standing habits. It's the only way to achieve the impossible in the Christian life. It really is that simple!

But some people don't like simple. They prefer complicated and confusing. They especially prefer any method that makes them stand out from the crowd. Their prescription for living the Christian life goes something like this: "You tough it out. You bite your lip, stifle your instincts, and act like a Christian even if it kills you!"

Does that sound like fun? Not to me. Christ promised abundant life, but toughing it out and pretending to love your enemy when you hate his guts sounds depressing and deceitful; the kind of program that comes from hell instead of heaven. No wonder some people reject religion! Who wants to live carrying a bag of wet cement on their back? Jesus said, "The truth shall set you free." He certainly wouldn't prescribe something as utterly dishonest as pretending to be something we're not!

Fortunately for you and me, on that fateful Thursday night, the last night before His execution, that isn't what Christ told His disciples to do. Instead, He said the secret involves a simple agricultural principle involved in the growing of grapes. "I am the Vine," He said, "and you are the branches."

Every gardener knows that if a branch is broken off its vine, it will soon wither and die. The vine supplies what sustains life for the branch and for the leaves and grapes it bears. And just as branches can stay alive only while they stay connected to the vine, so we can remain spiritually alive only as we stay connected to Jesus, the Vine. The Today's English Version of the Bible states it in language that is clear and easy to understand:

> Since you have accepted Christ Jesus as Lord, live in union with him. Keep your roots deep in him, build your lives on him, and become stronger in your faith, as you were taught. And be filled with thanksgiving (Colossians 2:6, 7).

How do we actually do that? How do we make sure that day in and day out, we don't lose our connection to Christ?

The way Amber and I stay connected is rather simple. Just as we couldn't have much of a marriage if we didn't spend time talking to each other every day, we can't really have a meaningful relationship with Jesus if we spend time with Him only once a week in church. So, we spend an hour with the Lord every day.

Here's how it goes: Every morning, we find a quiet corner of the house and talk to God. We tell Him what's on our agenda for the day, and we ask Him to enter our hearts, to subdue and crucify the evil desires of our sinful nature, and to forgive us for our sins and mistakes. Next we thank Him for His grace and goodness, we ask Him to bless others—especially our enemies!—and we tell Him about any challenges or problems we're facing and ask for His guidance and intervention. Then we open the Bible to Matthew, Mark, Luke, or John and read about the life and teachings of Jesus. Some days we make it through only a couple chapters; other times we read a lot more. As we read, we try to pay particular attention to the way Jesus treated people.

Amber and I have been doing this for many years, and we've made an exciting discovery: We've found that Jesus never came down hard on people who were having problems with a weakness in their lives. Sure, He drove the moneychangers from the temple and called the scribes and Pharisees "hypocrites" and "poisonous snakes." But those words of criticism were directed toward the members of the power elite of His day. He was especially vigilant against religious leaders who used their reputations and influence to bilk the common people out of their money in the name of God.

But as we studied the Gospels for ourselves, we found that every time Jesus encountered people with problems that left them with a guilty conscience and low self-esteem, He treated them with dignity, compassion, and love. More than that, He opened the door for them to walk away from their sins and into a fulfilling new life of salvation by faith.

Back then, there weren't so many people addicted to drugs as there are today. But Christ treated braggarts, prostitutes, alcoholics, and thieves as if they were the sons and daughters of God. And that's what they became through their association with Him.

Jesus still treats people that way. It doesn't matter to Him whether we're rich and famous or poor and unknown, upstanding citizens or criminals behind bars, sober or drunk, moral or immoral—He loves us all with a redeeming, transforming love. He calls each of us to turn to Him for repentance, forgiveness, and salvation.

When Amber and I first tried spending an hour a day with the Lord, it seemed like a lot of trouble. It also seemed like a very long time. But we had to be honest with ourselves, and that meant admitting that somehow we always manage to find time for what we really want to do. Whether it's watching TV, talking on the phone, pursuing a hobby, or going shopping, we always do what we value the most. So we decided to spend time with the Lord whether we felt like or not. And guess what? We soon found that the rewards far outweigh the effort.

As I recall what the Lord has done for me, I'm amazed at His patience. Time after time, He tried to break through to me, but I was too busy making a living, watching a game, or getting high. So He waited until I was ready.

The Spirit knows who and where we are. Silently, invisibly, He keeps track of the movements of our souls—not so He can condemn us for our sins; He does it so that He can save us when we're ready to admit we need help.

He watches while we fumble around trying to conquer our deep-rooted habits and addictions on our own. He listens when we promise to try harder. He's there when we get it right every once in a while, and He's still there when we kick ourselves for getting blindsided by the same old temptations that have brought us down before. He's there the hundredth time that happens; He's there the millionth time it happens.

Why is He always hanging around us like that? Because He knows that sooner or later we'll either tell Him to leave us alone forever or come to realize that the issues of life are way too big for us to handle on our own.

And what does He do if we come to that point and ask for His help? When I finally admitted I could never conquer my addictions without Him, the Holy Spirit reminded me that I am the reason God sent His only Son to die on the cross. He died for you, too! He died in agony for us, because of us, and in our place.

I'm a singer, not a theologian. I don't pretend to comprehend all the mysteries of faith, let alone to communicate them to anyone else. But I know—I have found to be true in my own life—that spending an hour a day with the Lord keeps me connected to the Vine.

Does this devotional practice add anything to what Christ has already done in His atoning death on the cross?

Absolutely not.

Is it some kind of do-it-yourself program to make us more acceptable to God?

Not at all. But it does give the Holy Spirit the opportunity to bring us into the Lord's presence on a daily basis so that we can experience His love, His power, and His healing—not to mention His friendship.

To grow spiritually, we must have an environment like that. As we encounter God day after day, the Holy Spirit performs the subtle, yet profound miracle of transformation in our lives. When we stay plugged in to Christ; the Holy Spirit does the heavy lifting. When we come just as we are, He changes our motives.

Is it easy?

Often, but not always. Sometimes I'm tempted to sleep in and let our devotional time slide. Once in a while, I do. Sometimes my mind wanders; sometimes I don't particularly want to spend time with the Lord, especially if I'm feeling a bit rebellious. But day in, day out, whether

I feel like it or not, I make it a practice to meet with the Lord. Then, despite the ups and downs and fits and starts, the connection survives, and my soul thrives in Jesus.

What about you? Are you perfect yet? Have you conquered all your bad habits and brought every impulse under control—even your thoughts, desires, and dreams? Or do you, like me, struggle and falter more than you care to admit? Give the hour-a-day plan an opportunity. Try it for a month and then a year. Better yet, make it a habit for the rest of your life. Most people waste an hour a day watching commercials. Why not invest your time in something that really matters?

An hour a day keeps the devil away better than anything else on earth.

Chapter Twenty-Nine

From Druggy Dreams to Goose Bumps

Satan is never happy when one of his prisoners is suddenly set free. So he does what any general would do in a time of war: he sets a plan in motion to recapture his former slave.

The first indication I had that the wolf was knocking at my door was when I started having lurid dreams about using drugs again. These dreams were realistic beyond words. I would wake up shaken and scared, convinced they were real.

Amber and I talked it over. We both feared that in a weak moment I might backslide. After all, my former drug buddies still lived in the neighborhood, and the stuff was readily available on the street. We decided I needed a change of environment.

The Fiji Islands are about as far away from the Southern California drug culture as you can get in this world. We didn't go there to find Christ. Praise God, He had already found us! We went there to escape all the familiar faces and places that conspired together in a variety of subtle spiritual and psychological ways to bring me back into captivity again.

I've already said that I haven't used drugs since the day I received Christ on the bathroom floor, but I wouldn't be telling the whole story if I said it hasn't been a struggle. As this book goes to press, it's been more than fifteen years since my deliverance from drug addiction, but the devil maintains an active solicitation program designed to flatter or intimidate us into falling. His ultimate objective is our eternal destruction; he doesn't want to be alone in the fire. But fortunately for the Christian, the Holy Spirit is more vigilant than Satan. If He weren't, none of us would survive.

When we got to Fiji, I found a wonderful new environment for the next stage of my recovery. The islands are beautiful beyond words! Try to imagine bright blue skies, balmy trade winds, regal palm trees, incredible beaches, and some of the nicest people on the face of God's green earth. If that doesn't do it, perhaps you should go there and see for yourself.

The church members on Vanua Levu showered us with love and affection. Their straightforward honesty and humble lifestyle set them apart as the most genuine group of people I have ever met. In an effort to make us feel welcome, they began having church in the home where we were staying.

These church services weren't exactly what I had in mind when I agreed to move to Fiji with Amber. I was looking for space and time to sort things out with the Lord. And even though these folks were very understanding, they persisted in turning our home into a place of worship.

When the services started, I'd usually hang around for a while, then slip out and find a place to smoke. Even though God had delivered me from alcohol, marijuana, and cocaine, my addiction to nicotine was still very much intact. That was fine with me; compared to what I'd been through with drugs, cigarettes seemed like the epitome of mild.

Once in a while, however, I'd stick around and listen to the church services. And before long, the warmth of the worshipers' praises and their love of Christ completely engulfed me. I was drawn in hook, line, and sinker. Good thing, too. God had something wonderful in store that I never would have imagined for myself.

"Why don't come with us next Saturday morning?" someone would say. "We go down to the marketplace and sing for Jesus and share our faith."

The idea didn't sound particularly appealing to me. I never thought of myself as much of a musician. I'd always been an athlete, not a singer. But I did know most of the songs. Amber's cousins had been coming over to the house with their guitars, and I had learned "For Those Tears I Died," "Amazing Grace," and a few of the other tunes they sang.

"I'll think about it," I said. The truth was, I didn't want people to think I was some kind of Jesus freak. I thought religion was a private matter and that church should be held behind four walls, not out on the street corner. But my conscience started to nag me about it, and before I could say why or how, there I was, following them to the market one fine Saturday morning.

At first I just stood around and listened. I thought I was too cool to join in. But while they may not have been the most talented singers in the world (trust me, they weren't!), their enthusiasm was definitely first class. Before I knew it, I was joining in and singing with all my heart. I loved Jesus, too, and if they were going to stand there and sing at the top of their lungs, I would, too!

What happened next was a little bit embarrassing. People around us stopped whatever they were doing and began to listen. The volume had doubled when I began to sing. Soon I discovered that I was singing solo. The rest of our group was merely humming the harmony. Then it finally hit me: People were stopping to listen to me.

By the time we sang a couple more songs, we had a pretty good crowd. I don't remember if I was flattered or just plain shocked, but whatever it was, I just kept on singing. When we finally stopped, one of Amber's cousins took the opportunity to preach the gospel to the assembled crowd.

After his sermon, several people came up to tell me how much they had enjoyed my music. At first I thought they were just being nice and trying to make me feel good. But as the compliments kept coming, I began to wonder if perhaps God had given me a gift and this was His way of letting me know that He wanted me to use it.

To test that theory, I went with them again the next Saturday morning. Sure enough, the situation repeated itself. Before long, I was working with the group to expand our repertoire, and the next thing I knew, I was actually looking forward to Saturday mornings at the marketplace. Using my newfound gift to glorify God and seeing the people respond to the music gave me a very good feeling. I began to wonder if perhaps God was planning to use my voice to help spread the good news of salvation on a wider scale.

For some reason, the idea gave me goose bumps!

Chapter Thirty

Restoration in the Son

When we first arrived in Fiji, I considered myself more of a tourist than one of the locals. After all, I had lots more money than they did, and I was much taller than most of them and far more sophisticated. So I thought, anyway.

It didn't take me long, however, to get over all that. Thank God, too! While living among the Fijians, I learned that they have qualities that money and education can't procure. They genuinely care about strangers and tourists, and they possess a humility and generosity rarely seen in the hustle of modern life.

Don't get me wrong; I love the United States! I'm a flag-waving American who served his country in the military. I believe in the values our flag represents. But sometimes when I fly in to Los Angeles after spending time in Fiji, I'm overwhelmed by the contrast between the two ways of life.

In Fiji, the natural environment is beautiful beyond words, with vast expanses of pristine tropical wilderness. Over here, that's hard to find. In Fiji, the people are impoverished when it comes to material possessions, but they have warm, loving relationships with everyone they meet. Over here, we've got everything money can buy yet spend millions of dollars on psychiatrists because we're stressed, obsessed, and lonely. While we have taller buildings and better healthcare, the Fijians are some of the most contented people in the world.

When Amber and I ran out of money, we decided it was time to "go native." I didn't know what to expect, but before long, we both found our new lifestyle very much to our liking. It's such a light, carefree way to live. When we needed food, we either picked it from the garden or threw a net into the sea. It reminded me of what life was like during the time of Christ.

It also reminded me of what heaven will be like. These people treat others with the kind of love and care Jesus talked about. It was so beautiful to watch them reaching out to strangers as well as friends and offering to help whenever they saw any kind of need. The longer I lived in Fiji, the more I began to wonder how I could bring that same level of caring into my life. "Surely there must be something that Amber and I can do to help others," I told the Lord.

After a few months, I noticed that I was feeling better than I had for decades. The combination of freedom from drugs, stress, and worries had been good for me. I started wondering if Amber and I could open a live-in drug and alcohol rehab program right there on the islands. We did the math and figured that for much less than it costs to stay a month at a high-priced detox program in America, folks could fly to Fiji and live there for six months to a year.

Amber thought it was a great idea. In fact, she wanted to enlarge my vision to include caring for quadriplegics as well as addicts and alcoholics. We talked about that for several days, but finally decided it wouldn't be practical due to the difficulties of transporting nonambulatory folks across the ocean. We decided that if the Lord would open the doors, we would start a rehabilitation program for substance abusers and call it Restoration in the Son.

We began to make plans. Amber's sister Wilma and her husband, Timoci, agreed to let us modify a house they owned on a beautiful stretch of property overlooking the ocean. Amber and I would return to America, raise money to remodel the home to accommodate a group-living situation, and recruit a clientele.

When we got back to America, Amber and I flew into action. The Lord began blessing my newfound musical career from the moment we arrived in California. Before I knew what was happening, I was singing to large churches in different parts of the state every weekend. After my first CD came out, invitations started arriving from places like New York and Chicago. And everywhere we went, I told people about how the Lord had delivered me from drugs, saved our marriage, and given us the dream to launch Restoration in the Son.

Amber kept busy between concerts. Using her bedside telephone, she stayed in touch with the folks in Fiji and supervised the remodeling project that members of her family and other Fijians were doing. In a matter of months, we were ready to open our doors.

The way we set it up, the house was designed to accommodate six people at a time. But demand was greater than expected, so when we launched the program, we had eight residents. We drew the line at eight because we felt in order for it to succeed we had to maintain a homey environment.

Wilma was the hostess. She did all the cooking and cleaning and served as a friend and unofficial guidance counselor to the men and women whose bodies and minds had been shattered by their use of harmful substances. Uncle Timoci, as everyone called him, and Cousin Jack served as chaplains, encouragers, and prayer partners. The love of Jesus Christ was the focus and sweet influence that pervaded our rehab family.

Instead of living like pampered guests at a resort hotel, program participants all took part in manual labor every day. Although Westerners often look down on physical labor, it's actually a great healer when done in an environment of sunshine, fresh air, and natural beauty.

Some of the residents raised a garden and helped put wholesome food on the table. Others planted flowerbeds and kept the lawn and grounds in picture-postcard condition. Yet another group helped a blind lady in the neighborhood by mending her roof and mowing her lawn. And one of the participants, a fireman by profession, helped the community by teaching fire-prevention and first-aid classes.

For their part, the townspeople contributed to the success of the program just by being themselves. Their warmth and love enhanced the cordial atmosphere that helped the stressed bodies and tense minds of our program participants learn how to relax. Before long, personalities that had been hidden under clouds of drug-induced depression and fear began to blossom again. All that outdoor exercise, clean air, fresh food, Bible study, prayer, and love worked wonders.

Our success rate was unbelievable. In the five years that Restoration in the Son operated in Fiji, the majority of our residents returned home after six healing months and became productive, sober members of their communities. Some stayed as long as a year.

On one of my tours in the States, a gentleman approached me after a concert with an interesting question. "Why go all the way to Fiji?" he asked. "I've got some property you could use in Lolo Springs, Montana. I think it would be suitable for your purposes."

I told him about the fresh air, friendly people, and natural beauty of Fiji and explained that the islands had been so instrumental in my recovery.

"Why don't you come up to Montana and look things over?" he responded.

Why not? I thought. *This might be the answer to our prayers.* My singing career had taken off so much faster than anyone could ever have imagined that Amber and I were finding it harder and harder to commute back and forth to the Islands. Perhaps Montana would prove to be a good compromise.

When I got there, I was stunned. The area was magnificent! And the property had 264 acres of breathtaking mountain scenery, with three or four streams of crystal-clear water. It had a large swimming pool heated by natural hot springs, a spacious lodge, a country store, and twelve guest cabins, each with its own hot tub.

Clearly, we could accommodate a much larger group in Montana than in Fiji, and our participants could save the cost of trans-Pacific airfare as well. When the owner made us a very generous offer, it seemed like the Lord was opening the door. We prayed over it, thought about it, and decided to go for it.

Soon we opened the facility and operated it successfully for nearly a year. God blessed our efforts during that time, and three troubled but precious individuals came to know the Lord. All three were delivered from a life of addiction and chaos. It was a joy to watch them be baptized into the life, death, and resurrection of our Lord Jesus Christ.

After that year, however, the owner died, and his family decided to sell the ranch. We were very disappointed. It had seemed so clear to us that the Lord had directed us to this hallowed place, yet we knew He never closes one door without opening another.

In the years since Restoration in the Son closed its Montana operations, Amber and I have stayed in touch with our former program participants. One letter we got particularly warmed our hearts.

"I don't know what you did to John," the mother of a former resident wrote. "He wakes up early in the morning. He studies his Bible, and he prays for everybody. He is kind and considerate—a pleasure to have around. Thanks for giving us back our son. We have been praying for him for over thirty years."

As we said Goodbye to Montana, we kept our eyes wide open to discern which way the Lord would lead us next.

Chapter Thirty-One

Clearing the Air

Before I tell you what happened next, I better backtrack to share the story of how God used two men who couldn't speak a word to tell me it was time for me to stop smoking.

I met the first guy in a crowded grocery store in Ventura, California, on the Fourth of July, 1993. The place was packed with shoppers who, like me, wanted to make sure they had everything they needed for America's great festival of freedom.

Amber and I had just returned from Fiji and were about to open the rehab center in Montana. We were still not entirely clear what the Lord had in mind for us, so we started asking for guidance.

We were led to a beautiful church and started attending regularly. The pastor was a godly man, and the people were warm and friendly. It didn't take long for Amber to decide she wanted to be baptized and join the church.

I'll never forget the day she was baptized. It was my privilege to carry her into the baptistry. Baptism by immersion involves the momentary lowering of a person under water to signify that this person has chosen to follow Jesus and have his or her sins washed away. The person comes up from the water to begin a new life of faith.

Before the minister baptized Amber, he told the story of how she came to know the Lord. After that, one of the leading men of the church, a doctor in the community, rose to add his testimony about Amber's injuries and recovery. While this was going on, I was standing in the water, holding Amber, and noticing that she was getting a little bit heavy. But I was noticing something else, too. The Holy Spirit was trying to get my attention with the message that I needed to follow the example of our Lord and join my wife in baptism. *I love Jesus, too!* I said to myself. *How come I'm not getting baptized?*

Three weeks later, I was.

I'm sure that to some people it must have seemed like a spur-of-the-moment decision. But it was really the result of a process the Holy Spirit had been directing for years. As a child, I had always been aware of God, thanks to the wonderful influence of my aunt and other godly relatives. But as I got older, I resisted His love and did pretty much whatever I pleased.

After my life-changing encounter with Christ on the bathroom floor, though, I not only wanted God in my life but also wanted to give Him the very highest place in my affections. It was going to be me and my Lord and nothing between us! Under the guidance and control of the Holy Spirit, I had been set free from drugs and alcohol and everything that bound me to Satan and his lifestyle.

But had I really? As I thought about it, I realized there was one more link in the chain that held me at least partially in the kingdom of darkness, as Satan's spiritual empire is known. That link was tobacco.

Unlike drugs and booze, God hadn't taken smoking away from me in one short step. He did keep reminding me that smoking kills, though. To be frank, I knew that was true. I had heard horrible stories of lung cancer and emphysema, and I also knew I wanted to serve God with all my heart. So I made up my mind to quit.

That worked for a while. By trying very hard to resist the impulse to smoke, I sometimes managed to go without cigarettes for a few hours—sometimes even for half a day.

But no matter what I told myself or how hard I tried, I always ended up totally overwhelmed by the craving to smoke "just one more." I'd sneak away and light up, and the next thing I knew, I'd be reaching for another pack. And despite my best efforts to hide what I was doing, I never fooled Amber.

"You really need to give up those cigarettes!" she scolded. "They'll ruin your singing voice." Then she'd remind me that I might get lung cancer and that God would hold me accountable for destroying the musical talent He had given me.

Talk about a guilt trip! It wasn't exactly what you'd call positive reinforcement, but I knew she was right. I also knew, however, that I didn't have a clue how to go about breaking the habit before it broke me.

"Yeah, yeah, yeah," I would say. "I'm gonna quit." And off I'd go with a fresh load of resolve, only to feel it vanish like thin coastal fog beneath the hot summer sun the moment I thought of having another cigarette.

It seems ironic to me now, as I look back, that I didn't just come to my senses one day and realize that in breaking my addiction from drugs and alcohol, God had already set me free from addictions far more difficult to overcome than tobacco. Had I thought about that, I could have come to the conclusion that since He could do that for me, He could deliver me from smoking, too.

But I didn't see it that way. Instead, I saw only the daunting challenge of giving up smoking and said to myself, *I'm gonna conquer this thing if it kills me!*

Fortunately, the Lord intervened or it might have done just that!

There I was, standing in line at a Vons grocery store, waiting for my turn at the check-out counter. The tabloid headlines were their usual obnoxious selves: "300-lb. Man Gives Birth to Twin Goats," or something like that, and I was bored silly. Then an elderly gentleman came shuffling over and started talking to me. Why he picked me I hadn't a clue. "Had to have my voice box removed," he said in the terse mechanical cadence of a robot. "I smoked too many cigarettes and got throat cancer."

Whoa, I thought to myself. *This is too weird for words. That's exactly what Amber's been warning me about.*

Why did he tell that to me? I wasn't smoking, and I didn't even have a pack of cigarettes sticking out of the pocket of my shirt. I was just buying groceries.

The elderly man didn't explain why he'd chosen me to be the recipient of his startling disclosure. He just ambled away and disappeared into the crowd of shoppers. And I stood there with a head full of questions, wondering what on earth was going on.

The line moved forward, and now I was only one or two positions away from the cashier. I placed my items on the conveyor belt and turned around, and there he was again. He said again, "I smoked too many cigarettes and got throat cancer." This time he didn't mention that he'd had his voice box removed. And then, just like the first time, he turned around and walked away. I hurried through the check-out process and headed for home.

"You'll never believe what just happened to me!" I told Amber the moment I burst through the door. She listened intently as I recounted the bizarre incident in the supermarket. Then she said something I'll never forget: "Perhaps God is trying to tell you something. Perhaps that wasn't really an old man at all, Michael. Maybe that person hooked up to a voice box was an angel sent from heaven to deliver a message from God just for you."

I'll never know until I get to heaven whether or not God used a man with cancer or an angel in a very convincing disguise, but He definitely got through to me. Even though I've been back to that same store dozens of times, I've never seen my friend again. The Lord works in mysterious ways!

The second man who couldn't say a word was my beloved uncle. I was back in Chicago a short time later to visit my relatives. There, to my shock, I learned that dear old Uncle had recently undergone the very same surgical procedure as the mystery man at Vons. Unlike him, however, Uncle couldn't afford the electronic talking device and had to strain mightily to force any words to come out.

Try as I might, I couldn't hear a word he worked so hard to say. Poor Uncle! He finally got so frustrated that he grabbed a pencil and paper. "I got throat cancer," he scrawled on the page. "Too many cigarettes!"

It broke my heart to see Uncle suffering like that. It also broke through the last invisible barriers that chained me to the curse of nicotine addiction. When I got back home, I gathered up my cigarettes and threw them all away.

Praise the Lord, I haven't lit up since.

Chapter Thirty-Two

In the Recording Studio

People are always asking me where I learned to sing. They're usually surprised when I reply that I've never had a lesson in my life.

I've always loved music. When I was a boy sitting in church, my Aunt Margaret sang in the choir. She sang like an angel. I used to love to close my eyes and listen to the music that poured forth from her soul like a mighty river of love and devotion. It seemed I was in the very presence of God.

I wasn't the only one affected that way. People were often moved to tears when Aunt Margaret sang the story of Jesus. I sat there and dreamed that maybe one day I would become a singer and have people listen to me as intently as they did to my dear aunt.

But the years flew by, and I forgot about the power of music. Besides homework and school, basketball and girls filled my days. My plate was full. Nevertheless, something happened my senior year of high school that reminded me—if only temporarily—of that childhood dream.

Ms. Herman, the music teacher, organized our class into a choir to sing a few numbers for graduation. I wondered why she put me up front, but I didn't give it a lot of thought. During the ceremony, we put our hearts into the music and gave it everything we had. Ms. Herman was impressed. After the program, she pulled me aside. "Michael," she begged, "I want you to promise me you'll do something with that gift you have for singing. You might want to take a music major in college."

"Sure, Ms. Herman," I said, a bit surprised. "I like to sing. That sounds good to me."

I don't know how long I remembered that promise—probably no more than an hour or two. There were parties to attend and goodbyes to be said. And then I was off to the United States Navy for some big-time adventure and excitement.

It wasn't until years later that God directed my path toward music again. After the surprise concerts at the marketplace in Fiji, Amber and some of our friends began to suggest that I ought to cut a CD. The idea sounded intriguing, but was the Lord really in it? Perhaps we were just running ahead of Him into delusions of grandeur.

Amber and I talked it over. There were many obstacles—among them, the facts that we didn't know anything about the music business and we didn't have any money. If this was really God's will, He was going to have to open the doors. So we got down on our knees and prayed for a long time. Then, independently, we each came to the same conclusion: Music was God's will for us, but we were going to have to step out in faith.

That was scary! We didn't know much about living by faith, but little by little, things began falling into place. We discovered that a man ran a small recording studio in his home there in Fiji. Although the price he quoted was very reasonable by industry standards, it was still a lot of money for Amber and me.

The man said he would expect payment the day we picked up the finished CDs. Even though we didn't know where we would find the money, we said OK.

In what was either just a coincidence or the result of the Lord's engineering, Amber's sister Ida flew in from England the very day we were scheduled to pick up the CDs. We were happy to see her. But our anxiety about the money must have affected our welcome, because she asked what was wrong. So Amber confided our dilemma to her.

"I've got the money," Ida said. "I'll pay for Michael's CD."

Talk about affirming our faith! We hugged each other and praised the Lord. And then, just as soon as we recovered our composure, we drove to the studio and paid cash on the barrelhead.

Turns out the CD wasn't that great, but it got our feet wet in the business. Because I'd been in the studio and seen how the process works,

I began to feel confident that this was the path God was calling us to take and that faith was the only way we could walk it.

When we got back to California, Amber and I became deeply involved in our new church and made several close friends. Some of them would bring their guitars to potluck dinners the church sponsored. After lunch they'd play and I'd join them in song. And as in Fiji, so in California—everyone complimented my singing and encouraged me to believe that God had given me a very big gift and was calling me to use it to praise His name. That was exactly what I needed to hear!

Over the weeks and months that followed, I began to take my singing seriously. I could feel my voice maturing and growing stronger, and I realized that God was blessing me for His honor. I felt humbled and pleased.

As the requests for me to sing started coming in, Amber enthusiastically encouraged me to accept. She soon took on the task of artist management, something she knew next to nothing about. But that's never stopped Amber from doing anything she wanted to do. She has a great gung-ho attitude and goes after everything with all her might. I could never do what I've done without her.

Before long, people started asking for tapes and CDs. Unfortunately, we soon discovered that the quality of the recording we made in Fiji didn't compare to what was available in the States. But it's pretty amazing there was even a studio in the islands. Cutting my teeth in such humble surroundings was a great blessing—I probably would have felt intimidated had I walked into one of the multimillion dollar studios of California or Nashville for my very first recording session.

Anyway, Amber and our friends urged me to make another CD. "We should be able to find a top-flight studio around here," they insisted. "After all, we're in Southern California!"

That sounded great in theory, but money talks in the recording industry, and we didn't have any. And somehow, even after all that the Lord had done in conquering all the other insurmountable obstacles in our lives, a subtle form of unbelief crept in and loomed up before my eyes as the biggest dilemma of all. "You'll have to help me with this one, Lord," I said, with hardly an ounce of faith in my voice.

Of course, God came through for us again. When our friends from church heard what we wanted to do, they stepped forward in faith. "We think we can help," they said. "God has given you this great gift, Michael, and you need to put it to work. We'll take care of the expenses."

So, in just a few weeks, Amber and I were holding the first copy of *Songs From the Heart* in our hands.

That did it! When I saw the unbelievable success God brought to that first professional-quality CD, I lost all doubts that this was what He wanted me to do. Like David, the shepherd, I was under divine appointment to make music for His Majesty the King of kings and Lord of lords!

By His matchless grace, I intend to sing praises to His holy name forever!

33

The Lady I Love

Amber is an absolute jewel! Despite all we've been through together, she's always there for me and always seems to know just what to say.

Take my choice of music, for instance. As my reputation began to expand, Amber started hinting that maybe I should branch out a little. "Ethnic music is great," she said, "but you might be limiting your audience by not singing anything else." Her British-influenced upbringing in the Fiji Islands had exposed her to a greater number of diverse musical influences than I had been exposed to in my childhood on the South Side of Chicago. "There's a lot of beautiful new praise and worship music coming out," she added. "Maybe you should check it out."

Black people don't sing like that, I thought to myself. But the more I considered it, the more it seemed I should give it a try. Before long, I found I could relate to several new-to-me musical styles, including classical, country/western, Caribbean, folk, and the grand old hymns of the church.

Our singing ministry has grown to the point where I'm currently booked more than a year in advance. At each weekend concert, I share our testimony of how the Lord Jesus Christ saved our lives in the accident, delivered me from the horrors of drug addiction, turned our marriage around, and now gives us the opportunity to share our faith with people around the world.

While I get to go on stage and sing my heart out for the Lord, Amber has chosen to take upon herself the far more demanding and less glamorous aspects of our ministry. While she usually travels with me, occasionally she prefers to stay at home with the family. But regardless of whether or not she comes along, she handles all the details of scheduling, bookkeeping, concert management, and recording contracts. I couldn't even begin to do this without her.

The story of how a quadriplegic woman manages to run a music ministry from her home is interesting in itself. Every morning, after serving Amber her breakfast in bed, I help her bathe and dress for the day. Then I straighten the sheets and covers, carry her back to bed, and support her with pillows. With a TV tray serving as a desk and all her files, banking documents, and other papers nearby, our bed is suddenly transformed into an office.

Then Amber flies into action. One minute she's on the phone to Jamaica, arranging the dates for a concert. As soon as she's done with that, she calls the airline and makes reservations for two. Next it's on to the hotel reservations. An hour later, the trip's all set, so she does the accounting or checks the graphics for a concert program.

Her day at the office usually comes to an end at five o'clock in the evening, but not always. If she's coming with me on the tour or if there's a recording session coming up soon, she may work late into the evening. If not, she's either folding clothes, chopping vegetables, or helping one of our grandkids with their homework. She's a great teacher and mentor to them.

In addition to being the love of my life, Amber is my right arm. I love to watch her at work. She's so cheerful and professional, and she brings a wide-ranging expertise to the challenges of organizing my life. Despite the fact that I can't help feeling sad every so often because of her injuries, I feel a very powerful sense of pride in the way she does her job. The Lord knew I would need a strong, supportive wife to help me stay focused in my life and musical career. Her background in banking and the airline industry—as well as her intelligence, common sense, outgoing personality, and quick wit—are exactly what it takes to make this ministry a success.

But what I like most about the way Amber does her job is the way she treats people. We receive calls from all over the world. Regardless of the purpose of the call, Amber treats the caller with kindness and respect. Often when I walk into the room, I hear her comforting someone with warm, encouraging words of faith or praying for them over the phone.

There's a lot of pain and despair in the world, and Amber is one of God's frontline soldiers in the battle to share the good news of healing and salvation through Jesus Christ.

Whoever coined the slogan "Behind every successful man is a hardworking woman" must have had Amber in mind. I can't even begin to tell you how much I love and cherish my wonderful companion. I can hardly wait to watch her smile as Jesus instantaneously restores her to full mobility on the day when He makes all things new. I'm looking forward to heaven!

In the meantime, I'm thankful that Amber said Yes to me. Thankful that she never gave up. Thankful for her love and her earnest, insistent prayers. Thankful also that she showed me the Way.

I don't deserve her, but I thank the Lord for her every day!

Chapter Thirty-Four

You Don't Have to Be Superhuman

I hope it doesn't sound like bragging when I say that God has done some extraordinary things for Amber and me. He has blessed us far beyond our wildest expectations. Sometimes, as we review the evidence of His providential kindness to a boy from the South Side of Chicago and a girl from the South Pacific, we can hardly believe what He's done.

Let me share another story that highlights, once again, the fact that the Lord has always provided for us. This one took place shortly after we first came back from Fiji in 1989.

We got word one day that a well-known evangelist was going to hold a major crusade in our area. Amber and I were very excited and imagined ourselves listening with rapt attention as he preached the timeless message of Jesus and His power to save.

A week before the series began, the evangelist spoke at the morning service at our church and called for members of the congregation to volunteer to help with the logistics of the meetings. At the close of his presentation, the deacons handed out cards with boxes people could check to indicate whether they wanted to help by greeting folks as they came in, showing them to a seat, or collecting the offering.

Since the evangelist and his wife were both professional musicians, I didn't see any point in letting them know I could help with the music. But Amber and a few of our friends urged me to write "music" on the card, so I did and signed my name.

A few weeks later, the telephone rang. The voice on the other end of the line sounded weak and distant, but when I heard the name, I realized it was the evangelist. "My wife and I have laryngitis," he explained. "We're able to talk, but neither of us can sing. I see from the card you filled out that you're a musician. Can you help us?"

"I'll be glad to," I replied. "But I don't have very many songs in my repertoire."

"That's fine," he assured me. "We'll leave it in the hands of the Lord. I'm sure He'll provide."

And He did. Just like the widow in the Bible whose meager supply of oil and flour never ran out, I had plenty of songs to sing even though the illness of the evangelist and his wife lingered for the remaining three or four weeks of the crusade. Whenever I needed another song, the Lord made sure I got one just in time.

As the series came to an end, the evangelist came by to thank us for helping with the crusade. "You were a godsend!" he beamed. "In fact, we were wondering if you would care to join our team. We travel from city to city and could really put your gift of music to work for the Lord."

Amber and I talked it over. "You might never get another opportunity like this," she said. I knew she was right, so we said Yes.

For the next few months, we helped out with the music as the evangelistic team traveled to dozens of churches. As a result, I started getting invitations from pastors who wanted to know if I might return to their church for a complete concert. We were elated!

One day Mark Finley was in the audience as I shared my testimony and sang. Mark is the speaker and director of the popular *It Is Written* television ministry. After the service, he sent one of his staff writers to ask if I would like to be on TV.

Me? I thought. *On TV?* I had never imagined such a thing. I could handle a live audience well enough, but the idea of singing on TV seemed strangely intimidating.

"I can't do that," I replied.

When the writer asked why, I couldn't find a solid answer.

"Pastor Finley and I were impressed that the Lord could use your talents on our program," he persisted.

That line of reasoning got through to me. Amber and I had promised to follow wherever God might lead us, and the more I thought it over, the more it seemed He might be asking us to walk through this door. With many misgivings, I finally agreed.

The taping sessions went smoothly enough. I chose some of my favorite songs, and after a few hours in the studio, we completed two separate programs. It was a completely new experience, but the staff were supportive Christian people who made us feel at home, and Amber and I were touched by their kindness and encouragement.

Once the first episode aired, orders for our CDs started pouring in from all over the United States, Canada, Australia, the West Indies, and Europe, and soon our concert calendar was booked for the next several months. And before we had time to adjust to all this, calls started coming in from other American ministries, including Three Angels Broadcasting Network and *The Quiet Hour* on TV, as well as *The Voice of Prophecy* radio broadcast and *100 Huntley Street* from Canada.

Why did all this happen to us? I wish I knew. I know it's not because we're better Christians than other believers, because we're not. But in an age when the media glamorizes rehab programs that promote esoteric, manmade theories and psychological alternatives to the simple gospel of salvation by faith in Jesus, the improbable story of how the Lord rescued two generic sinners from the hopelessness of addiction and despair is urgently important and must be told.

Why? Because people are searching for answers today. As I write these words, millions of people are struggling to break free from alcoholism, drug addiction, sexual perversion, compulsive gambling, eating disorders, and countless other forms of enslavement. Very few people can afford to take a month or two off work and spend thousands of dollars at a high-priced rehab center. But even if they could, there are no guarantees. Despite the most sophisticated medical technology and innovative psychiatric interventions, the majority of people who seek help from these sources never attain freedom from addiction. So, lives are being destroyed, homes broken, and futures wasted because people don't know that it isn't up to them to save themselves.

"Pull yourself up by your own bootstraps!" is the world's answer to the problem of addiction, but it's the biggest lie ever told. "Solve your own problems" is the noble-sounding foundation principle of every rehab philosophy in the world that isn't based on the gospel. But underneath it lies the same dangerous deception the serpent told Eve in the Garden of Eden: You can be your own god.

And where do these spin-doctored slogans of the New Age self-help movement lead? To the revolving-door syndrome. To years of expensive therapy. To false hopes for a permanent recovery that somehow never materializes. To ongoing depression and decades of dependence on numbing medications with powerful and destructive side effects. Far too often the ultimate destination is a trip to the morgue years ahead of schedule.

These ideas sound so good, but they don't open the door to freedom because they can't open that door. Jesus Christ *is* the Door. At the cross, He conquered the cause of all the brokenness, addiction, and chaos in the world. The blood He spilled on the rocks at Calvary is the only industrial-strength soul cleanser known to humankind.

As the Door of freedom, Jesus is open to you. No matter what you've done or how far you've traveled on the road to disaster, your Savior and Creator is calling you, at this very moment, to come and receive forgiveness for your sins and power to overcome. He invites you to let Him conquer the inner demons you could never defeat on your own. He is offering you a life of freedom and dignity and peace with God and yourself. As an old hymn asserts, "It is no secret what God can do. What He's done for others, He'll do for you. With arms wide open, He'll pardon you. It is no secret what God can do."

Amber and I have walked down both sides of Addiction Avenue. We nearly lost our lives. That's why we're reaching out to you. You can come to Christ. He can set you free. It's as simple as that.

How can you come to Christ?

By crying out to God with all your heart. Tell Him you've tried to reform your behavior and turn your life around. Admit to God that it hasn't worked. Then tell Him what you've needed to say for a long, long time: "Save me, Lord Jesus! Save me because I cannot save myself."

Once you do, you'll discover that you don't have to be superhuman to go free. You just have to know Someone who is.

Chapter Thirty-Five

Amber's Mental Diet

At my concerts I do most of the talking. But every now and then Amber has something to share. When she does, it's always worth hearing. People come up to her afterward and thank her for sharing her story without glossing over the difficult parts. Some can relate to the part about her crying herself to sleep before I found the Lord. Others know someone who is disabled. They find that Amber's willingness to discuss her challenges gives them greater understanding and insight. Still others are disabled themselves; they thank her for telling the truth.

Since I'm not qualified to discuss what it's like to live with a disability, I'm going to let Amber do the talking in this chapter. She has chosen to reveal the secrets of what she calls her "mental diet"—the thoughts she feeds on to maintain her equilibrium. I think you'll enjoy what she has to say.

People don't realize what a great loss it is to have a spinal-cord injury. It affects your life in ways you would never imagine. The things I miss the most are everyday things I used to do, like putting my arms around my husband and dancing with him. And even though I thank God that I still have my husband, the loss of daily routine is difficult to accept.

But God is good, and eventually, through a lot of tears and prayers, we manage to deal with the loss and rebuild our lives. We pick up the pieces, add some new ones to the mix, and create a new way of life. The past is gone, but, through Jesus, there is hope for tomorrow.

I set goals all the time, arranging and rearranging my priorities. Despite my disability, I feel I can still enjoy a quality of life that is the equal of— and in some cases perhaps even better than—that of my nondisabled peers. So long as I have a telephone, a pen and paper, and the ability to use my voice, hands, and brain, I can direct my life. Because I have the Lord, I'm glad to be alive.

Today I can honestly say that I'm the best-cared-for quadriplegic in the world. Not only has the Lord kept the promise He made years ago in Fiji when He assured me He would take care of Michael, but I also get bubble baths and candlelit dinners! Isn't God wonderful?

Sometimes when trouble comes, when it seems that every way I turn is blocked or insecure, I am reminded that God is the Creator of everything—and that He never fails. In times like that, I try to remember what the Lord says in Scripture, "Be still and know that I am God."

I acknowledge that God's wisdom is guiding me in all matters and at all times. I often still my thoughts by turning my attention away from the situation at hand and waiting upon the Lord. I've been practicing this since the accident, and I have found, time and again, that it brings peace of mind and great joy. I smile when this happens because I know that in God's presence I find the reassurance and understanding that I seek.

Along the way, I've come to treasure a number of verses of Scripture. One of my favorites is Isaiah 40:28, 29:

> Have you not known? Have you not heard? The everlasting God, the LORD, the creator of the ends of the earth, neither faints nor is weary. . . . He gives power to the weak, and to those who have no might He increases strength (NKJV).

In the next verse, the prophet alludes to the fact that there are circumstances of life so challenging and demanding that even the young wear out and faint with exhaustion. He concludes, in verse 31, with an assurance that has encouraged me time after time in the past fifteen years:

> Those who wait on the LORD shall renew their strength; they shall mount up with wings like eagles, they shall run and not be weary, they shall walk and not faint.

To the person who has suffered great loss, to one who is going through a time when nothing seems clear, I would offer another promise that continues to bring me hope. It's found in Psalm 18:28: "You will light my lamp; the LORD my God will enlighten my darkness" (NKJV).

One of the things I've come to realize is that when I look at the storms in my life and keep dwelling on the problems, I get overwhelmed and they become monsters. At times like that, I connect with the ever-present Spirit of God. Regardless of what issues we're facing in our lives, we need not become discouraged by what we see or overwhelmed by our circumstances. The truth is forever settled in heaven: "I will not forget you. I have engraved you on the palms of My hands."

It is our privilege to wait on the Lord in faith and glad expectation for the things He has promised. This is what the Lord says in Isaiah 49:8: "I will answer you, and in the day of salvation I will help you" (NIV).

I take that to mean that God has a designated time when His promises will be fulfilled and our prayers will be answered. No matter what our natural senses tell us—even if we think God isn't making sense!—we are to hold on and keep believing God. We are to wait in faith for the day of God's favor and salvation.

On Calvary, God gave us His only begotten Son. How could He forget us when Jesus is seated on the throne in heaven with those nail prints still visible in His hands? God is so wonderful; He really meant that part about engraving us on the palms of His hands! Instead of destroying us for our sins, He chose to forgive us.

We're not always like that. Sometimes we decide to lash out and get even. But when we do that—when we choose not to forgive; when we decide to hold a grudge or refuse to let go of painful memories or nasty rejections from long ago—we hurt ourselves more than anyone else. We punish ourselves by closing our hearts.

At first, after the accident happened, I used to tell myself, "I'll think about it tomorrow." Everything was "tomorrow." Now I just write down everything that's troubling me and prioritize it all. Then I try to work on solving the most urgent problems first—not through positive thinking or mind control, but through the Scriptures.

Today, I'm up more than I'm down, primarily because I know God has healed my soul, and my legs weren't going to take me to heaven anyway. I'm not so concerned anymore about whether I'm ever going to walk again. I just want to be happy for this day. That's why I do what I do; I've learned to be content in whatever situation I'm in.

Does that mean I never feel sad? Of course not. Whenever I face a new challenge, I try to deal with it right away. Sometimes, if I find it's too painful or mind-boggling to resolve immediately, I cry a little. Or maybe a lot. I find there's something healing about tears. I used to be ashamed to cry, but a couple years ago I discovered that after I cry, if I get up and brush myself off, I feel good. So I've learned that it's OK to cry.

It's OK to face your fears, too. I'll never forget the day I confronted one of mine. We were at a potluck dinner after church, and Michael was scheduled to sing. About five minutes before his concert I discovered—to my dismay and embarrassment—that my leg bag was leaking. "Oh, God!" I prayed, "Do I still have to go up in front of all these people and give my testimony?"

The next thing I knew someone was wheeling me into the men's restroom (the door of the ladies' room was too narrow for my wheelchair), and I cleaned myself up. I can't begin to tell you how embarrassed I felt! Fortunately, I found a blanket and draped it over my legs just before I was wheeled to the front of the sanctuary to share the story of how God spared my life and gave me the courage to forgive and go forward in grace.

The Holy Spirit blessed my presentation, and afterwards, a number of people told me the Lord had used my story to touch their hearts. And not one of them knew about the minor emergency He had just gotten me through.

Those of us who live with disabilities face little crises like that all the time. How do we deal with our problems? By getting stressed out? Becoming frustrated? What can we say when we're mad at the whole world and everyone is to blame? We can always look to the Lord.

How is it with you? Have you stopped to smell the roses lately, or sat and watched a beautiful sunset? How about listening to the song of a bird or the laughter of a child? How long has it been since you read to someone who can't read or comforted someone who is ill or brought a smile to someone who's sad? These are among the richest blessings of life, yet most of us don't enjoy them nearly as often as we can or should.

I've just got to share one more story about something the Lord has done for me. This one is just too good not to tell.

The day I flew back to Michael after he told me how the Lord had come into his life was December 25, 1988. I was so glad to see him that Christmas Day! Eight months later, however, I was feeling very homesick for Fiji. When I left my mother's house, I was told I was ungrateful to those who were trying to take care of me. Of course, that hurt a lot. But now I wanted to tell my mother that I loved her. However, she didn't have a phone. So I sat there, wondering what to do. I glanced at the clock; it was ten o'clock in the morning.

Among the things that were troubling me was the fact that although I'd been praying that my mother would come to trust in the Lord, I hadn't seen any evidence that anything spiritual was happening in her life. Around two in the afternoon I had this overwhelming urge to pick up the phone and call my sister Sharon. To my surprise and amazement, Mother answered the phone!

"What are you doing there?" I asked her.

"I'm standing here dripping wet!" she replied.

"How come? What happened?" I wanted to know.

"I just returned from the beach. I got baptized today," she replied.

Remember what I told you about coming to grips with the fact that it's OK to cry? Then you can guess what I did when I got off the phone!

Satan took aim to destroy my life. He took away my ability to walk. He stole my husband—there was a very long time when I thought Michael was gone for good. He used my best friend to betray my trust and steal my joy. He even turned my own mother against me.

But Jesus came through just as He promised He would. He gave me a new life and restored my marriage. My husband is now my brother in Christ, my mother is my sister in Christ, and Michelle is my best friend in Christ. And on top of all that, God has promised that one of these days, I'm going to walk on the streets of gold.

Better yet, I think I'll dance!

Chapter Thirty-Six

A Typical Day

Once again I'm going to let Amber do the talking. She's the expert when it comes to knowing what it's like to live with a spinal-cord injury. I'll resume my narrative in the next chapter.

When I first wake up in the morning, it's time for exercise. After Michael gets me up, he sets me on the edge of the bed for our "imaginary bicycle" routine. He holds on to my ankles and feet and helps me do a series of rotations as if I'm peddling a bike. This not only stretches my legs to increase blood circulation but also ensures that I get a full range of motion with each limb. After a few minutes, we move on to other stretching exercises. This part of our day is actually a lot of fun. It usually lasts from forty-five minutes to an hour, depending on interruptions.

Often the phone rings two or three times while I'm exercising, but we don't mind. We could just leave the answering machine on, but since we work out of our home—and since exercise, work, and play are all part of our life together—why not just pick up the phone and see who's calling? We have some great conversations at that time of the day.

Next on our agenda is a nice warm bath. If Michael gets distracted, he'll make it too hot—he loves hot water. However, my range of tolerance is set at a lower point than his. Since much of my body can't feel temperature, sometimes I'll notice my skin turning red, and I'll discover that I'm experiencing shortness of breath. When that happens, I stick my fingers in the water; they make an excellent temperature gauge!

When the bathwater is too cold, I experience muscle spasms. One time I had such strong back spasms that I actually hit my head against the tub. Ouch! I suppose we really should get a bathtub thermometer, but most of the time Michael gets the temperature right.

Why am I telling you all these details? Because most people don't realize all the everyday accommodations—some major, some minor—that must be made to handle the activities of daily living for a quadriplegic person. I've got to give Michael very high marks, however. He's a master at helping me do things I could never do for myself.

While I'm soaking in the bath water, Michael makes the bed and then prepares my catheter and leg bags. They don't have to be changed every day, but when it comes to matters of personal hygiene, I prefer more rather than less.

When I'm finished with my bath, Michael lifts me out of the tub, helps me dry off, and applies lotion if I need it. He doesn't have to do everything; I enjoy toweling myself as much as I can. Michael's very good at caring for me. In the sixteen years that he's been my caregiver, I've never had even a single bedsore.

The next stage is getting me dressed for the day. Michael brings my clothes and helps me into them, then seats me in front of the mirror. I can blow-dry my hair and comb it.

While I'm doing that, Michael's fixing tea, toast, and oatmeal or maybe scrambled eggs and rice for breakfast. He brings it upstairs to me, and once we've eaten, he goes back down and cleans the kitchen. Then he comes back upstairs and makes sure the tub, sink, and floor are clean and dry. Then he does any laundry, if necessary, and vacuums the floor. He's very efficient: At this point, we've only been out of bed for a couple hours, and he's already put in a full day's work.

While Michael finishes his chores, I spend time with the Lord. This is the best part of each day—the part where I get to talk to my best Friend and read His Word. Everything around me comes to a halt as I commune with God. He calms my mind, subdues my insecurities, and reminds me again of His love, wisdom, and power. I can't tell you what a difference our daily time together makes in my life.

What happens next depends on whether or not we have anywhere to go that day. If we don't, Michael brings me everything I need for the work I'll be doing that day: bills to pay, paperwork to file, letters and thank-you cards to write, etc. Once I get started, Michael takes care of his own showering and dressing for the day. Of course, the phone is ringing steadily by now, and before I know it, I'm talking with a friend, counseling a new believer, scheduling a concert, and/or making airline, hotel, and rental car reservations. Some days our bedroom/office seems like Grand Central Station, but I enjoy it. To be honest, I thrive on a challenge! Good thing, too. By the time the work day is finished, it's been eleven hours of hectic activity, and I feel tired, but happy.

On travel days, our schedule is crazy beyond words. Instead of getting up at a decent hour, we start the day at two o'clock in the morning. We go through the whole exercise routine, take a bath, and get dressed. Of course, I dress differently when I'm going traveling than I do when I'm staying home all day. When I'm dressed, Michael cleans the room. We don't leave it a mess because that's the way we'd find it when we came home after a grueling concert tour.

Then Michael carries me down the stairs, we pick up a rental car, drive to the airport, park as close to the terminal as possible, and then Michael lifts me out of the car and into my wheelchair. He doesn't use any kind of mechanical lift. We tried a Hoyer lift once but found that we get along better without it. So, as you can imagine, Michael's back is pretty sore by the end of the day. He has a bad back to begin with, but after getting me in and out of the car and wheelchair, he's had a real workout.

If we're flying to New York or Chicago, we might not arrive till eight o'clock at night. By the time we get to the hotel, we're exhausted. Of course, it's doubly tough in cold weather.

We face another set of challenges once we get to the church where he'll be singing. It seems like some of these buildings have eighty steps to climb. OK, I'm exaggerating a little; they usually have only fifteen or twenty. But by the time Michael carries me up the stairs and into the sanctuary for the concert, then back down again after it's over—and sometimes into the basement if they're having a potluck dinner—we're both worn out. I can't even begin to imagine how tired he must be! I just know it's a considerable strain on me, and I'm not the one doing the lifting.

Even so, just sitting up straight in a wheelchair takes more effort than most folks realize. It's difficult because I'm paralyzed from my chest down and from my elbows to my fingers. I don't like to sit flopped over, so all the time I'm in the chair, I'm pushing myself backwards. That becomes tiring after a while.

My paralysis has other disadvantages. One day, while using the blow dryer on my hair, I accidentally rested my elbow on a hot curling iron on the dresser. It was very hot, but I didn't feel a thing. About that time Michael walked into the room and said something smelled like burning flesh. I raised my elbow, and in the mirror I could see that the searing heat of the curling iron had burned a white mark so deep into my flesh that it almost reached the bone. I hadn't felt a thing! That was rather scary, but it taught me to look carefully whenever I use the curling iron or anything hot.

Sometimes people wonder why we're not very sociable after a long day of traveling and singing. Occasionally, we accept their invitations to go out to dinner or to take a sightseeing trip, and then we're almost too tired to smile. I suppose accepting our limitations and saying No when our minds and hearts want to say Yes has been one of the hardest things for both of us to learn.

I could go on and on about the challenges Michael and I face on a daily basis, but before I close this chapter, I want to say that we could never cope with this level of difficulty if we didn't have the Lord. We're both working a lot harder now than we ever did before the accident. What keeps us going is the realization that this is not our ministry; it's the Lord's. We enjoy what He's given us to do. He's promised to give us the strength to do it, and He's never let us down.

I know that one day I'll walk again. It may be here on earth or it may be in heaven—I don't know which. I've had people lay their hands on me and pray for my healing more than one hundred times. Some folks claim to have the gift of healing, and they accuse me of not having enough faith to believe that God is going to work through them to heal my body. I used to get upset when people would scold me for my "lack of faith," but I've learned to just smile and say, "Yes, if it's God's will, I will walk again." With or without doctors; with or without the laying on of hands. Perhaps now; perhaps not until "the trumpet shall sound."

Some day I will hear the Lord say, "Take up your bed and walk." Whether that happens in this life or the next is really not that important to me. I know that this life is only for a season, and the Lord is coming soon.

I'm content to wait on the Lord. He's given me the grace to be happy and content, and that's quite a miracle in and of itself.

Chapter Thirty-Seven

"Plant the Bulbs!"

One day I told Amber we had just been invited to dinner at the home of Herb and Mary Joines.

"Who are they?" she asked.

"This couple from Fillmore," I replied. "They're wonderful people; you'll like them. Let's just go."

When we arrived at their home, Mary looked across the street and said, "You know, I've been praying that you will buy that house over there. It's for sale."

Amber and I looked at the house, and I felt sad. Mary didn't know about our situation. You see, for years now I haven't had a full-time job outside of the house. I work for In-home Healthcare Services as Amber's caregiver. Aside from that, my only other income is from the sale of CDs and tapes. They pay the rent and put food on our table, but there's never enough money left over to save for a house.

"What a beautiful home," Amber said. Then, in an attempt to change the subject, she suggested that it would be a sin if the two of us lived in such a big beautiful house all by ourselves.

The dinner was lovely, and Mary and Herb are wonderful Christians. Mary is persistent, too. She invited us back for dinner another time. I didn't suspect a thing, but she had an agenda in mind. When we arrived, Mary suggested we all tour the house that was for sale.

It was huge! With more than twenty-five hundred square feet, two master bedrooms and three smaller ones, it was easily one of the biggest homes I'd ever seen.

"It has four bathrooms," Mary was saying, "and one has a whirlpool tub in it. The laundry room is upstairs and—"

No way! I thought to myself. *There's not a chance we could ever afford a house like this!*

But for some reason—it always seems like God touches my heart and I can't explain how it happens or why—I felt impressed to go talk to my son and daughter-in-law about it. So off I went to see Chris and Kathy.

My decision to talk to them was a miracle in its own right, because I had my doubts. *There's no way our son wants to live with me,* I was thinking as I headed to their place.

But when I got there, Kathy became very excited about the idea. "Don't tell the kids," she urged. "Don't say anything in case we don't qualify. We don't want them to get discouraged."

So we brought Kathy and Chris out to see the house, and they fell in love with it. But we all felt sad when economic reality set in. We didn't have any money, and the owner was asking for thirty thousand dollars down.

When we told him we couldn't afford it, he responded by saying, "Well, you can lease it with an option to buy. I'll give you six months to come up with the thirty thousand dollars. If you don't qualify in three years, you lose your thirty thousand dollars, and I'll take the house back."

At that point, everyone started thinking the idea was ridiculous. I thought so too. "We'll lose the thirty thousand dollars," we said. "It's just not worth it."

But Someone whose opinions are wiser than ours kept tapping at Amber's heart and telling her to go for it.

About that time, Amber and I flew off for one of our weekend concerts. When we got back, we found a notice in the mail from the government. It was a notice that Social Security had underpaid me by $4,000. All I had to do to collect the money was to sign an enclosed card and mail it in.

The next thing I knew, we got a check in the mail for four thousand dollars. Shortly after that, sales of my CDs brought in enough money to cover the balance of the thirty-thousand-dollar downpayment on the house. We were stunned and amazed. We had no doubt that the Lord was trying to tell us to use the money for the house. So that's exactly what we did!

It took a while to get used to living in such a big house. Amber and I took the bedroom with the whirlpool bath—a hot water bubble bath really helps her relax—and Chris and Kathy took the other master bedroom. The kids each have their own room, and I have a place to practice my music.

The next three years sped by. Soon Amber and I were facing the fact that our lease was about to expire and if we couldn't qualify for a loan, we were going to lose the thirty thousand dollars and would have to move out of the house.

So here we are, Amber thought. *The third year is approaching and I'm doubting the Lord. I'm looking at the finances and I'm thinking, "We're not going to qualify!"*

Six months before that Amber had ordered some flower bulbs from a mail-order nursery. She didn't order just a few of them, mind you; she spent two hundred dollars on bulbs! And then her faith really began to falter.

"I was afraid to plant them," she remembers, "because I started thinking, *Well, what if we don't qualify for a loan? If that happens, all that money I spent on the bulbs is going to be wasted.* I had already forgotten how we got the thirty-thousand-dollar downpayment on the lease in the first place."

Worry is seldom our friend. Worry tries to solve all the difficulties on its own without calling on the Lord. Late one night, worry had Amber in its grip and was giving her a good hard squeeze.

What am I going to do, Lord? she pleaded.

"Plant the bulbs!" came the reply.

Plant the bulbs? Lord, I can't plant the bulbs. We haven't qualified yet!

"Plant the bulbs!" He insisted.

The next morning, she called one of her girlfriends. The girlfriend came over, bringing her kids, and the whole entourage went out back and planted the bulbs.

Then Amber started doubting again. She called the owner of the house and asked for six more months to qualify for a loan. "Listen," he told her, "why don't I just give you twenty thousand dollars back, and you can go buy one of those new houses that sell for two hundred thousand?"

Amber thanked the man for his unbelievably generous offer—and then started thinking that something wasn't right. *He's willing to give us back most of our money so we can go to the bank and buy a house for two hundred thousand dollars. Yet we bought this house for two hundred and thirty thousand, and he already has the down payment of thirty thousand dollars. So why don't we just go to the bank and see if we can qualify for a loan to buy this house?* Amber made an appointment, went to the bank, and came home rejoicing. The Lord arranged things so we got the loan, and we've been living in that house ever since.

Amber and I could go on and on telling stories of the miracles God has worked in our behalf. She wants me to tell you about the time I got a nice pair of shoes for a dollar. As much as I'd like to, I'm getting hungry.

I think I mentioned this house has a wonderful kitchen. So if you'll excuse me, I think it's time for a sandwich . . .

Chapter Thirty-Eight

Friends on the Sea of Glass

As Amber and I speak to audiences all over the world night after night, our biggest hope is that our story will inspire others to call upon the name of the Lord and find salvation and freedom as we have.

Has it worked for others? Yes it has. Allow me to share stories of how God has intervened in the lives of a variety of folks who have attended our concerts and heard, through our music and testimony, the joyful message that Jesus saves.

On January 25, 2003, I got an email that reminds me that I'm not the only man in the world whose addictions have caused pain and suffering to the woman he loves. Rather than summarize it for you myself, I'll just quote it (with permission) as it stands:

> Hey Michael,
> I hope and trust that you are doing well. This is Kristy Woods from the Cayman Islands and I just wanted to let you know that your ministry is very appreciated. I was talking to a gentleman who just recently turned his life over to Christ, and amazingly, his background is very similar to yours. He was a very heavy drug user. He came home drugged up one night to find his wife asleep. He became so outraged that she was sleeping and not waiting up for him at 3:00 in the morning that he stabbed her three times in the back of her neck. It is still a miracle that she is alive. She is paralyzed from the neck down. She left him, but for the 16 years that they were separated after the

incident, she never gave up on him. She prayed for him every day . . . and like yourself, they are back together. The Power of God!! It's amazing!

He told me that after the concert, he wanted to meet you, but he had to get back home to his wife, and the foyer was too crowded. But he said that you were a great encouragement to him . . . I guess it's just to know that he is not alone in his struggle. Tears actually came to his eyes as he recounted his story. He still almost finds it hard to believe that God could love him so much that even through it all, God never let go of his hand. He said that if I spoke to you that I should tell you that he is praying for you and your family, that God will continue to bless your ministry. So I am passing on the message.

Take care and God bless!

Kristy

This story points out two important facts: The first is that drugs are dangerous business. I don't gather statistics on how many people die each year from drug-involved accidents, but the toll in loss of life, limb, and dignity is staggering. The best advice for everyone is don't start. You can't get hooked on something if you never start in the first place.

The second insight to emerge from the story is that the Lord can save even after the worst of tragedies. I rejoice that my Cayman Island brother did come to know the Lord. And I'm thankful that his wife never stopped praying for his conversion. Rest assured that Amber and I have been praying for them ever since we got the email.

Another changed-life miracle took place about seven years ago when I got a call from someone in Oklahoma who had attended one of my concerts and heard the story of what Christ did for me. The person on the other end of the line was very concerned about a relative, a construction engineer from Australia. Apparently, the man—let's call him Steve—had been drunk for several days and was holed up in a hotel in San Diego, unable even to answer the phone. Steve's relative asked if I would be willing to go down there to tell Steve about the Lord.

When I arrived at the hotel a few hours later, Steve was too drunk to answer the door. So I went downstairs and got the clerk to open it for me. We found Steve sprawled across the bed in a near-unconscious state of inebriation. When he finally did awaken enough to open his eyes, he wondered who I was and what on earth I was doing in his room. I told him about the call from Oklahoma, and eventually he agreed to come with me to a wonderful detox/rehab center that the Salvation Army operates in Carpinteria, California—a small town on the outskirts of Santa Barbara. I'll never forget the ride to Carpinteria: We had to stop every two or three miles for Steve to vomit.

Steve spent that night with the Salvation Army, but the next day he collapsed and had to be rushed to the hospital. The medical personnel reported that he would almost certainly have died had he stayed in the hotel by himself another day.

I'm almost afraid to tell you what happened next for fear you'll think I'm making this up. That's a risk I'm willing to take, however, because of what the Lord did. After Steve got out of the hospital, he returned to the Salvation Army facility. He gave his heart to the Lord there and completed their excellent recovery program. That was seven years ago. He's been "clean and sober in Jesus" ever since. Today Steve is involved in his own ministry back in Australia. Isn't it amazing what the Lord can do?

On another occasion, Amber and I met a quadriplegic gentleman—I'll call him Mike—whose condition is even worse than hers. Mike's wife brought him to one of our concerts in his specially equipped van. As he listened, he warmed to the message of the saving grace and love of Jesus, and he bought some of our CDs.

We lost touch with Mike until one day a few years later when his wife called to tell us the amazing story of what had just happened. During the intervening time, Mike had deteriorated medically and had to be hospitalized for an extended period. Instead of getting better, however, he slipped into a coma. The doctors warned Jessica (not her real name either) that he didn't stand a very good chance of ever regaining consciousness.

Jessica did everything she could to bring Mike around, but nothing worked. She talked to him, read to him, and invited friends over—all to no avail. Weeks went by, and Mike remained in a coma. Just in case something on television might capture his attention and cause him to snap out of the coma, she left the TV on day and night in his room.

The day the miracle took place, the TV set "just happened" to be tuned to a certain channel that "just happened" to be broadcasting a

Christian program. I "just happened" to be making a guest appearance on the program that day, and Mike "just happened" to hear my song. He "just happened" to recognize my voice and the song the Lord had "just happened" to give me to sing. Mike's recovery from unconsciousness "just happens" to be one of my favorite miracles!

I could go on forever with these wonderful testimonials of what the Lord has done, but I've got room for only two more. The first one was told to me by Chaplain Pam Scott—that's her real name!—who works at a prison for women in Norco, California. Here's what Chaplain Scott told me in a letter:

> I held my Sunday service in the women's gym because [it] could hold 250 women, and on the day you were to give the service, it was packed out.
>
> One of the women, after the service, told me later that she had come down to get your autograph and told you that she knew you before that day. She'd had a warrant out for her arrest and was in a hotel room waiting for her drugs to be delivered. She was flipping through the channels when she stopped at you singing "What Sin?" She said that "it was just like he was singing this to me, and I knelt down right there in front of that TV set, closed my eyes, and asked Jesus to forgive me and come into my heart. I then went right over to the phone and called my probation officer so I could turn myself in and stop the running. He told me that he couldn't get anyone to come get me for three hours, so I walked sixteen blocks to the police station and turned myself in. I have been here ever since."
>
> Thanks again Michael for coming to Norco, and for going on Channel 6 with me shortly afterwards.

At yet another concert, I met a young man who had been addicted to both drugs and hard rock music. Many people downplay the role of music in holding people to their addictions, but I know from firsthand experience that there is a definite link. Music bypasses the logic centers of the brain and stimulates powerful emotions. Who hasn't felt a rush of adrenaline after listening to certain types of music or noticed the calming, soothing effect of other types?

Anyway, this young man, I'll call him Tom, was hooked on drugs and on the music of Metallica. He played their songs night and day and found himself caught up in their lifestyle of sex, drugs, and bizarre forays into the dark world of the occult. But one day Tom found the Lord, and He set him free from all his addictions.

Today Tom plays my music instead of Metallica's. He says it makes him feel like the Holy Spirit is speaking directly to his heart, offering hope, comfort, healing, and power to stay faithful to the Lord as the melodies and words minister the love of God into the very parts of his brain where demonic music had played such a central role in holding him captive to the power and will of Satan.

So, God has used Amber's and my story to touch the hearts of Steve and Tom and many others. I'm looking forward to meeting them on the sea of glass when Jesus returns and spending eternity with them. There's another person I want to meet there too. In fact, maybe we can have side-by-side apartments in the mansion Jesus is preparing for us in the Holy City. Though Anna Withers is White and I'm Black, when she attends my concerts I often introduce her as my mother—much to the audience's puzzlement. Amber considers her a surrogate mother too.

It all started back in the early 1990s at a place called Ventura Estates, a retirement community owned by the Seventh-day Adventist Church in Newbury Park, California. This beautiful home for senior citizens is situated on eighteen acres of lawns and gardens, birds and squirrels. Amber and I were excited about singing for the residents.

After our concert, a lovely lady came up to me with a startling announcement. "God spoke to my heart while you were singing," she said. "He told me to take care of the two of you." I wondered what she meant by that last line. Before I had a chance to find out, she turned on her heel and left the room.

A few days later as I was going through the mail, a credit card fell out of an envelope that I was opening. Inside the envelope I found a note from someone named Anna. She introduced herself as the woman from the retirement home and said, "God is using you, and you are going to need this for car rentals, hotels, and other expenses. I know you'll use it wisely."

What a godsend! I can't begin to tell you how many times we've used Anna's credit card to enable us to appear in churches and schools all over the world. It isn't too much of a stretch to say we couldn't have done it without her. I'm not saying the Lord couldn't have provided for our needs without Anna because He is completely unlimited; and He's never let us down. But Amber and I both say, "Praise the Lord for Anna!"

In the intervening years, Anna has become a spiritual guardian to both Amber and me. The three of us have spent a lot of time together and become very good friends. Anna attends as many of our concerts as she can and always brings people with her. Most of them are people she's been leading to the Lord. And we call Anna several times a month—sometimes it's several times a week—to ask her to pray for someone in trouble or for Spirit-filled guidance on an issue of concern. We've learned that things happen when Anna prays!

It would be impossible for Amber and me to adequately thank Anna for all she's done for us. I'm convinced that God sent her into our lives just when we needed her the most. Thank you, Anna, for all your help. And thank You, God, for sending her to us!

I'm always amazed at what the Lord can do. I have no idea how many people He has touched through my story and songs, but I always remember it isn't me they're responding to. What breaks through hard hearts and brings hope to the hopeless is the simple, timeless story of the gospel of grace. The source of our freedom and the basis for our security and joy is the beautiful story of a God who loved the world so much "that He gave His only begotten Son that whosoever believeth in Him should not perish, but have everlasting life."

I love sharing the story of Jesus! I love to sing of the love that rescued me. I'm looking forward to being a part of that vast multitude that no man can number. When those mighty angel choirs sing, I intend to raise my voice along with theirs in praise and worship to the Man of sorrows who saved me by His grace.

In the meantime, I'll keep on singing. I feel humble when I realize that God is blessing others through the voice He gave me.

By the way, what are you doing for eternity? If you haven't invited Jesus to be the Lord of your life, why not do it now? There's plenty of room on the sea of glass!

Chapter Thirty-Nine

The God Who Made the Stars

When I was a little boy growing up in Chicago, the bright city lights prevented me from really seeing the stars. But as an adult, I've traveled to places where the stars gleam and glimmer like millions of white diamonds on a sea of black velvet.

I'm not a scientist, and I know next to nothing about astronomy, but I have a friend who really gets into it. I have to admit that some of the things he's told me about the size of the universe are pretty impressive— like the fact that the sun in our sky is 109 times bigger in diameter than the earth. Or that there are some giant stars in our Milky Way galaxy that are a thousand times bigger than that. I don't know about you, but I can't begin to comprehend anything 109,000 bigger than the planet we call home! My friend tells me that light travels at 186,000 miles per second. But our galaxy is so big that even if we could travel at the speed of light, it would take us more than one hundred thousand years to go from one end of the galaxy to the other. And this is just one galaxy among billions!

Suffice it to say, the universe is a mighty big place. In fact, the only thing bigger is God's grace. Regardless of who we are, what we've done, or why we've chosen to hide from Him, God's mercy and forgiveness are even greater than the infinite reaches of space.

Somewhere out there, in a place that the most sophisticated telescopes will never be permitted to explore, the One who loves us looks down on our tiny planet and whispers our names. If we listen, we can almost hear Him. Our Creator, the One who made this world dance on invisible waves of gravity and light, wants us to understand that we are not alone. He wants us to know that we mean more to Him than all the planets and stars, solar systems and galaxies put together.

God's love for us is the reason He voluntarily rode through the gates of Jerusalem on a donkey one Sunday afternoon, knowing that when He left the city five days later, He'd be carrying the cross to a hill where He would die for our sins. It's also the reason He is stretching His arms wider than the deep blue sky and saying, "Come home, child—I miss you. Everything is forgiven. Even though you were guilty, your sins are washed away in the river of My blood. Your future is secure. I love you. I need you! Come home."

You and I are invited to the grandest celebration in all of time and space. Everyone who responds will know music and laughter and endless joy. The food will be out of this world. Likewise the fellowship, the peace, and the fulfillment. And just for the heaven of it, our Host is offering eternal life as a free gift to all His guests.

God's throne may be trillions of light years across the universe, but if you're ready to say Yes to Jesus, the news will travel to His ears at the speed of grace. How fast is that? Before you even finish saying Yes, God will be cradling you in His arms of mercy and forgiveness and love.

At this very moment our Creator awaits your reply. To R.S.V.P., just say, "Thank You, Jesus. I had no idea You'd do something so wonderful for me!" Then get ready for an everlasting adventure with the God who made the stars.

If you've been blessed by his story, you'll be blessed by his music!

Set Free

The renowned baritone sings the praises of the One who set him free in this diverse album that testifies to God's redemptive power. From the traditional "Turn Your Eyes Upon Jesus," to the inspiring "Just For Me," this album transports the listener into the presence of the Almighty. Songs include: "I Miss My Time With You," "The Potter's Hand," "Above All," and "When It's All Said and Done."

CD: 4333003431

Other albums by Michael Harris:
- Glorify Thy Name (with Phil Draper) - CD: 4333003286
- A New Song - CD: 4333002801
- Glory - CD: 4333002391
- I'll Forever Lift My Voice - CD: 4333003169
- In Christ Alone - CD: 4333001908
- Jesus Loves Me - CD: 4333001904
- Merry Christmas With Love - CD: 4333002797
- Songs From the Heart - CD: 4333002480
- There's A Wideness - CD: 4333002484

And introducing Michael Harris's granddaughter, Kayla Tiaré Louis!

Little by Little

Following in her "Papa" Michael's footsteps, Kayla has released her first CD. Only eight years old when she recorded this album, Kayla's love for Jesus and her gift for singing come through with a sweetness that warms the heart. A spirited duet with Michael on "This Little Light of Mine," anchors a delightful album that includes the songs "Little by Little," "Angel in the Sky," "Stand," "I Am a Promise," "Big House," and others.

CD: 4333003394

All Chapel® Music CDs are US$15.98, Can$23.98.

Order from your ABC by calling **1-800-765-6955**, or get online and shop our virtual store at **<www.AdventistBookCenter.com.>**
- Read a chapter from your favorite book
- Order online
- Sign up for email notices on new products

Prices subject to change without notice.